THE OFFICE
ROCKSTAR
PLAYBOOK

Praise for *The Office Rockstar Playbook*

The Office Rockstar Playbook is a story of administrative excellence at its best! Debbie shares her story of stepping out of her comfort zone as she weaves in critical tips on how she succeeded by being all in. Her statement, "You won't know the outcome if you don't try" is spot on! This book is not just for the administrative professional; it is saturated with insights to help anyone transform and grow, professionally or personally. Rich in wisdom and courage with hints of laughter, this book inspires and leaves you ready to challenge yourself.
—SHEENA HOUSER-SMITH, Executive Assistant, Cisco Systems

I could not put this book down. Debbie shares so many great strategies and stories that are relevant, inspiring, and showcase what a true leader should do. Every executive and administrative professional should read it, as it maps out how to perform at the highest level while being a true strategic partner to our leader. Her book will become a go-to manual for assistants around the world.
—PAULA THIBODEAU, Executive Assistant, Government of Canada

I was floored by all that Debbie juggled and accomplished over her career. I had no idea how much CEOs rely on their executive assistants to make sure they can do an amazing job, and it was clear that she played a significant role in her CEO's success. Even more, I was blown away by her passion for developing other people in her field. The skills and tools she developed over the years aren't just valuable for other EAs. They're essential success skills for anyone who has a demanding corporate job or a business to run.
—CANDICE DAVIS, Breakthrough Success Coach

After reading *The Office Rockstar Playbook*, I sat down with my CEO and showed him the book. Not only did it validate my working style, it also validated my value as a leader on his executive team. Administrative professionals and executives alike will gain insights, knowledge, and a new perspective of the value of a true strategic partnership when both choose to rise

to the occasion. Whether you're an administrative veteran or have just landed your first support role, do yourself a favor and read this book. Run – don't walk – your fingers to your keyboard and order your copy today!
—JONELLE L. BURKE, Executive Business Partner and
Chief Administrator, Kountable

The Office Rockstar Playbook is an incredibly well-written book for all levels of administrative professionals. This book is a Bible we all need to have at our desk. Debbie talks in detail about extending far and beyond being an administrative professional; she focuses on being a true business partner. She's holding our hands on this journey which is so close to her heart! The book is hilarious, and the tricks and tips Debbie has openly shared are simply amazing. Besides the book, I highly recommend Debbie as a mentor. She is MAGICAL!
—DEEPIKA JAIN, Executive Assistant to the Head of People,
Chan Zuckerberg Initiative

The Office Rockstar Playbook is a page-turner. Debbie gives the reader an inside look at the world of CEO support, including the good, the bad, and the ugly of a stellar 26-year career. Debbie's writing made me feel as if she was talking to me one-on-one. The book is a wealth of information that can be beneficial to executive assistants (EAs), whether new or experienced. Debbie condensed this information into sixteen chapters, yet it speaks volumes. This book would also be beneficial to CEOs in gaining a better understanding of the day-to-day duties of their EA.
—ANGELA MOORE, Senior Executive Assistant, eSilicon Corporation

Debbie has written a remarkably insightful book that reveals the secrets of becoming a true business partner to any leader who manages teams or companies. Her lessons shared throughout the book will help administrative professionals and their managers think more strategically. This book should be 101 in every company where a senior leader is looking to hire an EA who can think strategically and tactically, connect with people, think three steps ahead, and be caring.
—PAMELA SHORE, former Executive Manager to Eric Schmidt, Chairman of the Board and CEO at Novell and Google

THE OFFICE ROCKSTAR PLAYBOOK

How I Leveled Up as an Executive Assistant and Helped My CEO Build a Multibillion-Dollar Company

DEBBIE GROSS

DEBBIE GROSS   CAMPBELL CA 2019

Debbie Gross
The Office Rockstar Playbook: How I Leveled Up as an Executive Assistant and Helped My CEO Build a Multibillion-Dollar Company

Published by Debbie Gross
710 East McGlincy Ln, Suite 103
Campbell, CA 95008
www.debbiegross.com

Designed by JBK Brand Design
(jbkbranddesign.com)
Cover photographs, Marcus Araiza for Atlas Studios
(atlaststudiosbayarea.com)

ISBN 978-1-7333847-0-4 (paperback)

I believe there is a voice inside of you that periodically calls you to move towards your true calling. The key here is whether you pay attention to it or not. Sometimes, when you do listen, you are not guaranteed immediate success. In fact, you may choose the wrong path as I did at certain times during my career. However, when you decide to take that risk—even if it doesn't pan out—you'll find that you discover a bit more about who you are and what you are really searching for. Taking those leaps of faith will lead you to your true calling. Keep leaping.

TABLE OF CONTENTS

FOREWORD
BY JOHN CHAMBERS

When Debbie asked me if I would write a foreword for her book, I didn't hesitate. Not because it was a nice thing to do for her (she knows I would do just about anything for her), but because it was a way to show my appreciation for all she did for me as my Executive Assistant of twenty-six years. Debbie brought immense value to me and was a true business partner throughout the majority of my career at Cisco. In fact, I strongly encouraged Debbie to write this book in order to share with the world what it takes to be an exceptional administrative business partner.

I arrived in Silicon Valley in 1991 to take a position with Cisco Systems as their Senior Vice President of World Wide Sales and Operations. While I was new to California, I was not new to sales nor was I naive to the critical role an Executive Assistant should play.

My expectations for what I needed in a support role seemed to be initially lost on the Cisco recruiter I was working with. They kept sending me applicants who were strictly secretarial in nature and average at best. Any one of them certainly could have done my expense reports and answered phones, but my expectations were much, much higher.

I was looking for an Executive Assistant who could think strategically and tactically, connect with people, and who could think three steps ahead and anticipate my needs. I was interviewing my seventeenth candidate (driving the recruiter crazy) when Debbie Gross walked into my office. Based on her answers to my questions, I knew right away that she had the skills I was looking for. Not to mention, our chemistry was great. I didn't need much time to think about it—I made her an offer that same day.

For twenty-six years – twenty years of which I was CEO of Cisco – Debbie was my right hand. Her deep understanding of what was important to me and, ultimately, the business; her ability to prioritize what came across my desk; and her incredible intuition, all helped me increase my productivity by 40 percent—enabling me to grow the company from $70 million in revenues when I started to $47.8 billion when I retired. Debbie was a critical link in the relationships that were most important to me, both personal and professional. She had an uncanny ability to connect the dots based on her knowledge and observations of what my business priorities and goals were. Debbie also brought fun and creativity to her role, which in turn helped me manage the stress of being a CEO, especially during the most challenging times.

Debbie earned the title of *Chief* Executive Assistant and was seen as Cisco's global administrative community leader, creating initiatives and programs that set her apart. She was no doubt my Office Rockstar.

What I've come to admire about Debbie is her ability to reinvent herself and train other administrative professionals to do the same. She led the creation, development, and implementation of Cisco's administrative training programs. Those programs elevated our administrative professionals to the top of the industry. I've received feedback from both CEOs and their administrative counterparts on the tremendous value her guidance and insights made on their own partnerships.

With her drive and passion, it's no wonder she's so sought-after in her industry. From Australia and Europe to India and Dubai, she's spoken at conferences, conducted workshops, and hosted leadership trainings that have impacted the lives of thousands of professionals. During Debbie's twenty-six-year career at Cisco, she raised the bar in terms of excellence for the administrative profession globally. She pioneered new administrative initiatives that taught key skills to differentiate average administrators from the great ones, because average is unacceptable if you want to make an impact. It is because of all of this that I nominated her in 2016 for the Colleen Barrett Award—one of the highest and most prestigious awards given in the profession. It was no surprise to me that she won.

If I were to describe Debbie's leadership style in three words, they would be "lead by example." She's the example of what administrative excellence is all about. With the passion and purpose she brought to her role in supporting me, she's what every CEO dreams of as the perfect match in an Executive Assistant. She *is* the Office Rockstar!

INTRODUCTION

T his story and my amazing career as an executive assistant began in March of 1991 when I accepted a position supporting John Chambers at a growing, seven-year-old technology company named Cisco. At the time, John was the Senior Vice President for Worldwide Sales. I was green, as executive assistants go, with little experience but lots of spunk and an "I got this" attitude. John was somewhat green too, having only recently been hired from Wang Laboratories. He had worked most of his career on the East Coast and was new to California and to Silicon Valley.

His West Virginia drawl and my Southern accent were a perfect combination. John's main responsibility in this new role was to level up the sales force for Cisco. By 1991, the company had revenues of $183 million and 565 employees but still functioned with a startup mindset. My job, as his executive assistant, was to help him manage that sales growth. Over the course of the next twenty-six years of working together (a rare occurrence in today's business world), my role with John became much more than just an assistant.

I learned so many valuable lessons throughout my career. The knowledge I gleaned from being a part of Cisco's growth (as of this writing, Cisco is an almost $50 billion company with more than 74,000 employees worldwide) includes tips, strategies, and stories I believe need to be shared.

Actually, when I decided to write a book four years ago, I planned to write about the human and humorous side of the administrative profession with stories that would bring a smile to your face. I finished writing it, submitted it to an editor, and was feeling quite proud of myself. Then John asked me an all-important question about that book as we sat over lunch on his patio in April of 2018. The question was simple. "Debbie," he asked, "what is the purpose of your book?"

That was when I realized that, while it was a fun read, the book didn't fulfill the purpose I wanted it to fulfill. John suggested that my book should be about excellence in the administrative profession and how I exemplified what a true executive assistant should be. It became clearer and clearer, as I listened to his feedback, that I had truly made his life easier, more productive, and more effective every day. I was his liaison with the internal organization and the outside world. My abilities stretched to include taking ownership, stepping into leadership, and creating administrative initiatives that were unprecedented in Silicon Valley.

John told me, "Debbie, you have done things no other executive assistant has. You've raised the bar on the profession, and you're seen as a leader in this role. You should tell the world how you managed it and how you made a difference in my life. Now *that* would be a compelling book." It was like a door had opened. I understood that this was my true calling and the reason for writing the book you're holding in your hands now.

Whether you are new in the administrative role, a seasoned executive assistant, or an executive, *The Office Rockstar Playbook* will give you all the skills, techniques, tips, and strategies I developed over my twenty-six years of working for the most amazing, highly energized, passionate CEO in the world. If you're in the executive assistant role, it's my hope that, as you read through these chapters, you'll discover new ways of adding value to your company. If you're an executive, this book will help you understand the full power of what an executive assistant can do for you when she or he becomes your true business partner.

1. THE EARLY YEARS

I grew up in Jackson, Mississippi, with my mom and dad and a little sister two years younger than me. Like all little sisters, she made me crazy, yet she was still my best friend. Life was simple. I loved playing all kinds of made-up games with my childhood friends in our yard and half the other yards in the neighborhood. I knew where every hiding spot was located within miles.

We often stayed out all day until either it got dark or we were called in for supper. My all-time favorite Saturday activity was going fishing with my mom and dad at the local reservoir. I could sit there for hours, eyes glued to the bobber at the end of my long cane pole, waiting for it to move up and down, which meant I had a bite. Fishing definitely taught me patience.

My mom was a stay-at-home mom, keeping house and making mystery casseroles (because she was cooking challenged), while my dad worked as a traveling salesman for a large lumber mill insurance company. We did fine, and with the money Dad brought in, we were able to eventually buy a new home, where I had my own bedroom. No more sharing with my sister. My life had just gotten even better. Being brought up in a Baptist family, my Sundays consisted of going to church and then heading to my grandparents' home for a big Sunday meal. Afterward, everyone would retire to the porch and claim their rocking chair for an evening of conversation. I would sit on the porch swing (my favorite place), and listen to my parents and grandparents talk about the weather, current events, and the latest happenings with the neighbors. Family communication always took place around the dinner table or out on the porch. You never wanted to miss those moments.

While we weren't a wealthy family, I never felt we were poor because my parents did their best to provide for us. Our clothes were handmade by Mom, including my Barbie dolls' outfits. I always had a goldfish in the fishbowl, and I had an amazing collection of colorful marbles, which I still have today. We didn't live a fancy life, but I was happy in Mississippi.

Then, as they are wont to do, the winds of change swept into our lives. We left Jackson in 1969 and headed for Kansas City, Kansas, as Dad was transferred there for his job. Having spent fourteen years in Mississippi, I was ready for change. Kansas City, here I come!

I spent my teen years in Kansas. I went to junior and senior high school there, learned to drive there, and found my first true love there—a boy named Bob. I also developed an itch for earning some spending money for myself above the little allowance I got at home—hence my quest for jobs like babysitting for neighbors and working at Smacky's Burger Barn. I thought I looked cool in my uniform sailor hat. At the local five-and-dime store, or what is now considered a dollar store, I worked my way up to cashier. It wasn't until I turned eighteen and asked my dad if he would buy me a car that I learned he wasn't rich.

My dad shared with me that, as much as he wished he could buy a car for me, he didn't have the money. He said he'd be willing to give me a thousand dollars (a huge sum in my mind and probably my dad's too) to put down on a car, but I would have to make payments until the car was paid off. I took out a loan, which he co-signed for, bought a used Toyota Corolla, and buckled down to make my payments every month. Life was good. I was driving the car of my dreams. When I think back now, I see my mom and dad instilled in us the importance of being responsible and accountable, especially when it came to money.

Right after my high school graduation, my father was transferred yet again, this time to California. I was devastated. I couldn't imagine any place better than Kansas, and I would be forced to leave my true love, Bob, behind. But the decision had already been made. I sulked in the back seat of our car as we drove all the way to California.

I was now a young woman, on the edge of nineteen, and I wanted out of the house. Much to my dad's chagrin, I was determined to establish my independence and rent my own apartment. He had always wanted me to stay home and go to college. As a C student, who struggled to get B's and rarely earned A's, I knew college wasn't for me. I decided, instead, that I would attend the school of common sense. It was time for me to look for a job that could help me pay my bills and live on my own under my own house rules.

At that time in my life, I didn't know anything about the executive assistant world. In fact, I had no idea what that role entailed, and I certainly didn't know what having a career meant. Just moving out of my parents' home as a single woman was a scary step out of my comfort zone.

My first real job was at a small advertising magazine called *Potpourri* (a paper thrown on people's doorsteps and eventually used to line the bottoms of bird cages). The goal was to sell as many ads as I could to earn commission. I had to do a lot of cold calling. It was a humbling experience, getting hung up on every day. Some days, I was great at connecting with people and getting them to buy; other days, it wasn't so easy.

What was even harder was having to periodically reach back out to those businesses I sold ads to and ask for their payment. I hated those days the most. It was tough asking for money, but if I wanted to get paid, I had to persevere and keep going at it.

Around this same time, I also learned what it meant to have a professional brand. I dressed like the typical twenty-something girl in jeans and, on several occasions, donned short dresses and miniskirts with high heels. (Remember the '80s?)

Two important events occurred that changed my perception of myself. One day, I walked around the corner to the break room and overheard two of my co-workers commenting on my short dress and how ridiculous it looked on me. I was ashamed, but I didn't want to give them the satisfaction of seeing it. I knew I had to somehow change my image from ridiculous to respectable.

The turning point came when my manager called me into her office to share with me that I needed to start dressing more professionally if I wanted to advance in my career. Well, that was it. I didn't like how my co-workers or my manager saw me. I needed to change. I immediately went to the nearest Dress Barn (my budget-friendly choice) to shop for a new look and a new me.

Although I had that job for four years, learning and developing sales skills and confidence in myself, there was still a voice in my head and heart that called out to me to reach for bigger and better things. I finally paid attention the day a young man came into our ad agency and walked up to my desk. He was placing an ad for a sales rep to help him sell medical supplies in the San Francisco Bay area. When I heard the salary for the job, that voice in my head said, *"Debbie, you can barely make your rent now. This is something you should take a chance on."*

Life offers us opportunities that we can either ignore or take a chance on to see where they lead us.

I ultimately took that chance and quit my job to go sell those medical supplies. However, I quickly realized I had just jumped off a career cliff. I didn't know what I was doing, had no knowledge of the medical field, and was truly unhappy in this new role. I quit that job after two weeks.

Taking this particular path didn't mean my inner voice was wrong. It just meant my spirit was telling me it was time for a change. As we often do during times of setbacks, I fell back on what I knew best and where I felt most comfortable. I asked for my old job back, selling ads. The advertising paper in San Jose took me back. It didn't take long for me to realize that I was right back where I had started: not making any more money and still not happy—yearning for something more.

The lesson I learned, and one I share with anyone in job transition, is to never go back to what you know and are comfortable doing.

There was a reason you left that job in the first place. I always encourage the administrators I coach to go forward even if the outcome isn't guaranteed. Transition is really about taking risks that help us grow. While selling medical supplies, quitting, and then falling back into selling ads wasn't my plan, those moves in my career showed me I needed a role in which I could further develop and explore my skills and expertise.

Too often, we settle into jobs and get comfortable, and as a result, we don't see the need to make any changes. I've observed many administrative professionals who stay in their comfort zones even when they're unhappy because of the fear of the unknown and the uncertainty that comes with change.

Sometimes we need to examine our level of happiness and fulfillment in our career and personal life. I started paying closer attention to times when I felt somehow unfulfilled. In my early years, I focused on having fun while working. That focus slowly changed to making more money and being financially comfortable.

As I began to find myself and my career direction, I had to hone in on and master a number of new skills. Sometimes, I learned through trial and error, which meant taking chances and making mistakes. I had to: 1) learn to listen to my inner voice (spirit or intuition); 2) gauge my feelings in terms of job satisfaction; 3) review where I wanted to be in my career; 4) step up and out of my comfort zone; and 5) take risks that didn't have obvious outcomes. It eventually paid off.

MAKE THE PLAY

1. There's a voice inside all of us that periodically calls us to move on towards our true calling. What matters is whether we pay attention to it or not. I was paying attention.

2. When we do listen, we aren't guaranteed immediate success, and in fact may choose the wrong path, as I did. It all leads us, ultimately, in the right direction.

3. When we take a risk, even if it doesn't pan out, we discover a bit more about who we are and what we're seeking.

2. I'M AN EXECUTIVE ASSISTANT: NOW WHAT?

By 1982, I had moved up in my career and was working as an office manager for a Japanese company called NMB, which manufactured miniature ball bearings for the booming disk drive industry. Two inside customer service representatives and a receptionist reported to me, and I felt like life was great. To top it off, Cory—my boyfriend of seven years—finally popped the question on Christmas Day of 1983 in front of my mom, dad, and sister. He handed me a tiny box that held an even smaller diamond and said, "I know I'm not Santa Claus, but would you marry me anyway?" I said "Yes!" Mom and Dad were very pleased and probably somewhat relieved.

Change was about to enter my professional life once again too. One day, a friend who I'd trained as a customer service representative called to tell me about a great opportunity at a company called Synesis, a Silicon Valley startup. It was an opening for an executive assistant. Initially, I was incredibly resistant. I laughed and said, "Hey, I'm an office manager and doing just fine here. Why would I want to move to a different company?" When she shared with me what the starting salary would be, I dropped my pen. I was happy in my job, sure, but my annual raises were two percent a year, at most, and at the rate I was going, I'd never see my financial dreams come true. As an office manager, I was experienced in just about anything that needed to be done in an office environment, so why not the role of executive assistant?

I decided to listen to my inner voice and take the interview. They made me an offer that very day, and I took it. That day changed the entire course of my career—all because I listened to the inner voice in my heart and head and decided to make a change.

Facing my fear head on and moving out of my comfort zone ultimately led me in the right direction and brought about amazing opportunities that otherwise may never have come my way.

Was it scary to take a new job in a startup doing something I had never done before? Hell yeah! But there I was, having just joined the ranks of the startup world, working as an executive assistant for two executives who I barely knew anything about. One of my executives was the Vice President of Manufacturing—a very laidback, grounded guy. He was always comfortable to talk to, positive, and easygoing. My other executive was the complete opposite. He was the Vice President of Engineering, a driven and extremely detail-oriented man, who commanded his engineering teams with an iron fist. He approached everything and everyone with intensity. In my first few days working with him, he asked me to re-staple the papers I was about to hand out to staff. The staples had to be at a perfect angle on the left side of the page. He was detailed to a fault, and he scared me.

I quickly learned that, in a startup environment, one wears many hats. I wasn't only the executive assistant; I was also asked to spearhead getting a new phone system for the office, manage the vendors, assist the new guy in sales, and sit in for our receptionist when she was out. I can honestly tell you I was completely naïve about my new job. I really didn't know what our company manufactured, nor did I know what my executives' goals or visions were. I was just trying to make things happen, every day, the best I could.

And then the bubble burst.

It started the day the company's major investor walked in the door and asked to see our CEO. I was handling the receptionist desk that day and didn't even know we had an investor. Our CEO wasn't there. Instead, Dennis, our Vice President of Human Resources, showed up in the lobby and spent the rest of the day in a conference room with our investor. It was a serious conversation.

Apparently, the CEO had been burning through the investor's cash at an alarming rate with no real sales to show for it. We were definitely in the red, and the investor wasn't happy at all.

The major investor was pulling out his interests in the company and demanded we close our doors. Our CEO was missing in action, and the news rippled through our small employee community like wildfire. The two executives I was supporting saw the writing on the wall and decided to quit. Employees were leaving, and I no longer had the role of executive assistant. Instead, I handled whatever needed to be done, including receptionist duties, employee communications, packing office files, and so on. I was the point of contact for whomever was left and whatever they needed done.

Dennis asked me if I'd be willing to stick it out and help him wind things down. Shocked and saddened about what was happening to me and the company, I really didn't want to stay, but he desperately needed some help managing things as key employees left. So I stayed. I was asked to assist in laying off a number of good people. I became the liaison between HR and our employees on the assembly line, who didn't understand what was happening. Ultimately, I became part of the team that closed up shop.

It was heartbreaking to watch people leave, but I stuck it out to the very day the chains were placed on the door.

 MAKE THE PLAY

1. As a good executive assistant, I had to learn to manage and adapt to two executives with different temperaments and styles. I had to balance their moods, needs, and communications styles every day.

2. I had to strive to do more than just the executive assistant role in order to continually develop my skills. I learned to embrace

tasks outside my realm of understanding, such as researching and purchasing the phone system or dealing with contracts, things I'd never done before. I didn't say it wasn't my job; I just dove in!

3. I should have made it a point to learn my two executives' goals and priorities, what the company manufactured, and what the bigger vision for the company was. I didn't know how to do that then, but if I had, I might have seen the writing on the wall sooner.

4. It's hard to remain resilient in times of change. I had to look at the good and bad and face challenges. It was yet another opportunity to grow personally and professionally. Assisting Dennis, the VP of HR, in closing the doors on the company and, sadly, closing the door on my first role as executive assistant, was probably the toughest thing I ever had to do. Through that process, Dennis became a good friend, who later helped me find another job.

There I was, among the ranks of the unemployed and facing the road ahead with multiple signs pointing in every direction. What had become clear was that the executive assistant's role was actually a perfect fit for me. I loved the fact that each day brought a different set of challenges and no two days were the same. I was the go-to person for everything anyone needed, and I enjoyed knowing that. I saw that being an executive assistant could actually be a career for me. To be the right-hand person working with executives who ran their organizations was exciting!

I decided to make looking for a job my job. Cory and I were a young, newly married couple, living in our first new home; financially, we weren't completely secure. I couldn't see Cory managing our financial obligations on his own, nor did I want him to. I prided myself on bringing in an income, so every day, I carved out time to look for a new opportunity.

I was sending out my résumé via snail mail back then. I didn't know anything about the internet, and there was no computer in our house. Can you imagine? It was the age of cell phones the size of shoeboxes (and I *did* have one of those). I checked the newspaper employment section every day. Based on the job posting, I tailored my résumé to highlight the skills I knew they wanted and then sent the résumé out via regular mail.

I kept a folder filled with all the newspaper postings and jobs I applied for and made time each week to follow up, which I hated doing. I was sending out five to six résumés per week, and it seemed like I would remain unemployed indefinitely. Then one day, about one month into my seeking-a-job campaign, the phone started to ring. It was great timing because I was beginning to lose faith that I would ever find my next job as an executive assistant. I was also losing faith in myself. (I have a feeling some of you reading this have felt that way when you're seeking a new opportunity.) Finally, I was getting requests to come in for interviews. (In today's world, phone interviews lead to video interviews lead to panel interviews before you even get to meet the person you would work for.)

I needed to prepare for this next phase of my job search because interviewing is a skill all its own. I got lucky one evening when I happened to meet a recruiter at a neighborhood party, and as we talked about the job market and the challenges of finding a job, he suggested I pick up *Knock 'em Dead: The 56 Toughest Questions You'll Get In an Interview*, by Martin Yate. I promptly went to the bookstore (no Amazon back then) and bought it. I read it and used it as my workbook for interviewing. It came in very handy.

My first interview was with the Director of Engineering for a fairly large corporation. I had to travel to several buildings in order to complete the interview process. I went to Building 1 to pick up paperwork and an identity badge, Building 2 to meet with my escort, and then to Building 3 where the director's office was housed. He greeted me warmly and showed me to his office. As we walked through the maze of cubicles, I took note of how quiet things were. Most of the employees had their heads down or were staring at their computer screens. It was eerily quiet.

The director and I had a great conversation, and as we wrapped up, he made me an offer. Right there. I wasn't quite sure what to do. Part of me was truly frightened that this may be the only offer I'd get, and I didn't want to remain unemployed. The other part of me helped me get my focus back. I let him know how flattered and appreciative I was, and that (my better judgment kicking in) I needed to review his offer and would let him know my decision by the end of the day. He smiled and piled on the compliments about my abilities. He was pressing hard for a decision, but I held my ground on my resolve to think it over first.

The director escorted me from his office to the front door, and as we wove through the sea of cubicles, I stopped and asked him, "So where would I sit if I were to take the job?"

He gestured to a small cubicle close to his office which, at that moment, was piled high with boxes and stacks of paperwork and file folders.

Oh boy. I walked back to Building 2 and then to Building 1 to pick up my car. As I sat there preparing to leave, I listened to my inner voice. If I took this job, I would be just another number in this huge corporation. I would be lost in a maze of cubicles in an obscure corner of the floor. It was way too quiet. In addition, I would be working for the Director of Engineering, not a vice president, the level at which I had initially provided support.

This was not the job for me. Even if it meant I would have to remain unemployed longer, I knew in my heart I couldn't take it. I called the director back the next day and thanked him again for giving me the opportunity. I explained that I really wanted to work at the executive level at this stage in my career, and I graciously declined his offer.

My focus was no longer on just having a job, but rather on establishing a career as an executive assistant, aka EA. I was still unemployed, but at least I'd aced the interview.

I was on to the next one.

"This is a great opportunity and a chance of a lifetime," said the recruiter. I was going to interview for an executive assistant's role supporting the CEO of a well-known Silicon Valley firm. A CEO! Never in my wildest dreams did I expect to shoot for that kind of opportunity, but armed with résumé in hand, I went.

It was the first of many interviews that week for the EA role in that company. I would have to run the interview circuit before I ever got in front of the CEO. I averaged at least two interviews a day and was on my sixth interview before I started to sense the culture of the company. In every interview, I asked each person what they liked about working for the company. The answer I almost always received was: "The pay is great!"

I also learned a lot about the term MBO (management by objectives), as it came up in each interview. The culture was driven by MBOs. No one seemed to be driven by passion or enthusiasm for their job, and I wasn't sure I liked what I was hearing. Finally, I was told I would have one last interview, this one with the CIO, or Chief Information Officer (I learned a new C-Suite term), before meeting the CEO. I was ready. For goodness sake, I had been interviewing so much I could do it in my sleep. The interview started off as they all had. I felt I was pretty well prepared with answers until he asked me to draw a Lotus spreadsheet on the whiteboard, using variables he'd give me.

My blood pressure shot through the roof at that moment. This wasn't in the interview book. I can remember to this day staring at the whiteboard, my back to the CIO, trying to put the marker on the board and realizing I had no idea what I was doing. Not only that, but I was beginning to feel as though I wouldn't enjoy working for the company. I didn't get the sense that people were actually happy working there—but they did get paid well. I turned around, faced the CIO, and said, "I apologize that I don't know how to do a Lotus spreadsheet. However, I'm a quick learner." He smiled and simply replied, "I'm sure you are." We walked out of the conference room together—he going his way, and my escort taking me back to the lobby. The next day, when I received a call from the recruiter, she was in tears. Apparently, I had done incredibly well in every interview with the exception of the interview with the CIO.

He hadn't been impressed with my lack of Lotus spreadsheet knowledge, and he was the deciding factor as to whether I would get to meet the CEO. It was a no-go. The recruiter shared with me that it had been hard to find anyone who could pass the initial interviews. I'd passed with flying colors on all of them but one. I thanked her and shared with her that, after thinking through the experience of interviewing with the company, it was probably not going to be the right fit for me anyway. After we hung up, I gave a huge sigh of relief. That job could have been disastrous for me in the long run.

MAKE THE PLAY

1. I needed to make looking for a job my job, and carve out time every day to do just that. Sending out lots of résumés allowed me to cast a large net that would ultimately bring in the right role.

2. I reviewed the job postings and tailored my résumé to highlight the skills I had that I knew they wanted.

3. Interviewing was a skill I needed to develop to prepare for the next phase of my job search. I bought *Knock 'em Dead* by Martin Yate and used it as my go-to resource.

4. It was important to listen to my inner voice in terms of what felt wrong about the job being offered. I had to be courageous enough to say, "It's not the right one for me." I had to be willing to hold out for what I knew I wanted for my career. Although I didn't need to jump to supporting a CEO, working for a vice president was my goal, and I stuck to it.

5. I began to think about the culture of the company I wanted to work for. I wanted to work with happy employees who loved their jobs, not those whose main reason for being there was the pay.

3. HELLO, JOHN

It had been a tough month. Although my husband, Cory, was financially assisting me, I was very proud of the fact that I'd always been independent and earned money for our family too. I was pulling funds out of my meager savings account and spending less to maintain some sense of independence. Every day, I perused the newspaper for employment ads that fit what I wanted in a job. (The days of the internet were just beginning, and there was no LinkedIn or Craigslist.)

Some days, I was disheartened because no one called me and, to be quite honest, I lacked the confidence to follow up with the companies where I had applied. The VP of HR, who I'd helped close down the startup company I'd worked for, gave me an interim opportunity working as a contractor in a new company where he had found employment. This helped me keep going and stay positive. He was paying it forward, and I appreciated his support and friendship. Knowing he recognized my skills and talents really boosted my confidence.

I finally got my lucky break in my job search when a recruiter from a little-known company named Cisco called me. He asked if I wanted to come in to interview for the executive assistant role supporting the Senior Vice President of Worldwide Sales. Having been out of work for a month, I was definitely interested.

The drive to Palo Alto, California, where the company was located, from my home in Campbell was at least forty-five minutes on a good day. What was I thinking? That said, I didn't want to turn down an interview, especially since I was among the ranks of the unemployed. So I drove the long commute on Highway 101 to Palo Alto.

Cisco had only three buildings, all located on the edge of East Palo Alto, which at that time was a very poor, crime-ridden neighborhood. Again I asked myself: What was I thinking? However, I was determined to go through with the interview process. Ultimately, I ended up doing more interviewing of the recruiter than he did of me. One thing was certain. I wasn't going to take another role with a company that didn't have a solid foundation. I also didn't want to be just a number or work in a place where employees were only there for the money (although that's always good to have). When I asked the recruiter, "What are your current yearly revenues?" I think he dropped his pen. He had never been asked that question before.

Two days after that initial interview, I received a call from the recruiter. He asked me to come back to interview with the Senior Vice President of Worldwide Sales. The SVP's name was John Chambers, and he, too, had apparently just started working for Cisco. I said, "Absolutely!" Immediately, I dreaded the drive back up to East Palo Alto. Was I crazy? The commute was going to kill me. What was I thinking?

My first interview that day was with the CEO's executive assistant, Sylvia. We met in the conference room, and she asked me the standard interview questions. Within about fifteen minutes, she put down her pen and said, "Okay, I've heard enough. You're definitely the right one, and I need you! I've been the interim support for John for the last two months, and I'm exhausted. He's interviewed nineteen candidates so far and hasn't liked any of them. Can you stay to meet John today?"

I said, "Absolutely." But I had some concerns. I waited for well over an hour to be interviewed, and I kept saying to myself, "Debbie, this commute sucks. This executive seems to be a real challenge, given how the EA to the CEO shed tears of joy when you said you would wait to be interviewed by him. Now here you are, waiting on pins and needles just to interview with this guy. What are you thinking?"

I waited well over an hour in that conference room before Sylvia came back to let me know John was available to meet me. With some trepidation, I followed her down the hall to John's office. What could this man be like?

He greeted me with a warm smile, and I extended my hand to shake his. Immediately, I felt a connection. We talked for almost two hours. His last question was: "How can I keep you motivated if you came to work for me?"

I promptly replied, "Money!" and then I smiled and said, "Actually, being recognized and appreciated."

He laughed and said, "Thanks for being candid!" He thanked

me for my time and said he would be in touch. As I walked out the door and headed to my car for the long ride home, I thought to myself, "I think that went well. He seems okay to me. Wonder what he's thinking?"

Forty-five minutes later, when I arrived back home, my husband told me I'd received a call from a John Chambers and that I should call him back. I immediately did, and John offered me the opportunity to come work for him at Cisco. I was absolutely thrilled at what he was offering in terms of a salary. It was at least 10 percent more than what I had been making—a grand total of $36,000 a year. Wow! This was in 1991, and in those days, that was a good salary. I knew I liked John; his style and his manner meshed with mine. Our chemistry was really good, so I blurted out, "Yes!"

I didn't even negotiate. I didn't know how to. I just knew this was the right role for me.

I liked being part of sales, so to be the Executive Assistant to the Senior Vice President of Worldwide Sales was a great fit for me.

I guess both of us were thinking the same way. This was the beginning of a partnership. I was going to work for Cisco as the new executive assistant supporting John Chambers.

MAKE THE PLAY

1. I never turned down an opportunity to interview, even if the job may not have looked like my ideal situation at the time.

2. I was prepared to ask smart questions about the company and the role. I made sure to interview the recruiter about the company just as much as he interviewed me. Some of the key questions I asked included:

   - What's the culture like?

   - What's the CEO's style?

   - What are their mission and vision?

   - Who are their customers? Are they global?

   - What are their annual revenues?

   - What attributes are they looking for in an executive assistant?

3. I learned patience is a virtue when I waited for that long hour to meet John for the first time. I could have just said, "To heck with it," and left. I'm so glad I didn't.

4. I was candid in terms of what I wanted when I was asked.

5. Sometimes what appears on the surface—the long commute and the poor neighborhood—are not what lies beneath.

These new ways of thinking changed my life forever. To land a role as an executive assistant for this young and growing high-tech company was an amazing opportunity for my career. I thought, "I got this!" But boy, was I wrong. John moved at lightning speed, and

I struggled just to keep up with him and understand all he required of me in my new role. I got my first shock on day one. In our initial conversation, he let me know he'd be leaving the very next day for two weeks of international travel to get to know his global team. He told me, "Oh, you don't have to worry about my travel itinerary this time. I already have it in hand. Just get a copy from Sylvia, and make yourself at home. I'll see you in a couple of weeks!" With that, getting to know John and his business priorities and making a good impression on him got a bit harder.

Day two, and John was now on international travel. I retrieved a copy of his travel itinerary and got my second shock. His schedule was full of meetings, morning, noon, and night. And they were taking place in four different countries. That equated to a new country almost every other day.

I asked myself what executive could possibly manage all that? And what executive assistant could possibly manage all that came with it?

That executive assistant, I realized, would be me. (Gulp!)

I noted the schedule and the time zones and who he was meeting with, and I kept an eye on the phone—the only thing on my desk so far since my computer hadn't arrived yet. That day, I received no calls from John. It was a weird feeling to have on my second day on the job. I decided to use the time to plan and to get to know some of the other executive assistants. I also needed to inquire about my computer. I was going to get one, right?

I walked around the office and introduced myself to other executive assistants and some of the executives. A few barely took a minute to smile at me, while others welcomed me warmly. Luckily for me, I made a good friend that second day. Her name was Rose Mary, and as it turned out, she had only been at Cisco for two weeks. She took me under her wing to show me what ropes she already knew and who was who in the zoo, and she became one of my dearest friends. We're still close to this day.

Without a computer, I decided I needed a plan of action or I'd go crazy. I was determined to learn everything about John even if I had to do it virtually. I remembered his exact words to me before he left: "Debbie, I trust you completely unless you prove otherwise, so my office and everything in it is yours." I began examining his files and everything else on his desk, including notes, phone messages, and miscellaneous bits of paper. My third shock: the exploration was like walking into a jungle without a guide.

John's desk looked like a bomb had exploded right in the middle of it. In fact, there were casualties: empty and half-empty Coca-Cola cans and a half-eaten bag of popcorn (his two favorite habits, I later learned) and cryptic notes that appeared to have been written by an alien hand on various pieces of paper. A stack of manila file folders with no labels lay on one corner of the desk, and he had no other folders or files in his desk drawer or filing cabinet.

I took a deep breath and decided to dive in and see what I could do to sift through, clean up, and organize things for this seemingly very busy executive. I read every phone message, making mental notes about each person and adding them to my contact list. I studied the cryptic notes to try to make some sense of the subjects, putting them into various piles according to topic. I brought in new file folders, typed new labels, and placed the folders in John's desk file drawer. I cleaned up everything on his desk. I even brought in a silk plant to give the office a homey feel.

When I finally finished, I stood back to survey my work. Everything was arranged in neat little rows and completely organized, and I patted myself on the back. As a bonus, I was just a bit more knowledgeable about John and his business. I left the office that day with a feeling of satisfaction. Little did I know that I had barely scratched the surface.

At the start of my third week at Cisco, my computer finally arrived. I was feeling a bit more at home when I got my fourth shock. John was back in the office, looking a bit weary from a grueling two weeks on the road. He sat down at his desk and immediately picked up the phone to start a conference call. Wait. What? No "Hi, Debbie. How are you?" I waited with bated breath for him to finish and acknowledge me.

Once he completed the call, John asked me to come into his office, and I was ready to hear: "Wow! What a great job you did in here while I was gone!" That did not happen.

Instead, he gave me a long list of action items, meetings, and phone calls he needed scheduled. When he finished, I had to ask, "Did you notice anything different in your office?" He looked at me blankly and said with all sincerity, "No. Should I have?" as he glanced around. Needless to say, I was disappointed.

John laughed and said, "Debbie, you'll learn that I'm not good at noticing the little things. I'm a big-picture guy. Just ask my former executive assistant, who brought in a couch and coffee table to decorate my last office. I didn't notice that for weeks! Great job of pointing it out. Thanks!" And off he went to update the CEO on his trip.

Then, I got my fifth shock. All the neat and organized rows of folders and messages on his desk were once again scattered to the winds, hit by what I soon fondly termed the Chambers tornado.

This marked the beginning of the new norm for me.

 MAKE THE PLAY

1. Being new to the company, I took the initiative to introduce myself to others, including executives, rather than wait for someone to do it for me. I gained an invaluable mentor and life-long friend in doing so.

2. Even though my executive wasn't around for my first two weeks at Cisco, I was determined to be proactive and learn about him through review of his files, notes, and messages. I started learning his business right away.

3. I realized that being disappointed because he hadn't commented or noticed me or what I had done for his office while he was away was a wasted reaction. It wasn't personal; it was John. I just needed more time to learn about him and his personal traits.

4. I began developing my roll-with-it attitude when various shocks and surprises hit me—and there would be many in my career with John.

The 1990s were the formative years in my career as an executive assistant for Cisco. I learned many career lessons that would stick with me for the rest of my life. About three months into working for John, I began to sense a change in his activities. This happened over the course of a few weeks. He had me scheduling lots of phone calls, and he popped in and out of our CEO's office. I'd just started to get my bearings in my new role. John's expectations were always very high for the people who surrounded and supported him, and I was no exception.

My number one goal each day was to just stay as much in sync with John and his needs as possible. That was no easy task. My executive was like a shiny pinball in a pinball machine, bouncing from one bumper to another bumper to another bumper—constantly changing direction. All I was trying to do was to keep the pinball from sinking into the wrong hole. I worked for a man who moved at the speed of light, and it was all I could do to keep up with him.

One particular Monday started out badly. I spilled coffee on my new suit during my commute to the office, and the stain was going to be a tough one to hide. I'd just started warming up my office chair when John came flying in—as he always did—indicating he needed to see me right away. Pen and pad in hand, I was ready. But not quite that ready. John explained that he'd need to travel that afternoon and would be gone for the week.

I'd have to reschedule all his meetings for the rest of that week. I stared at the pad and felt my blood pressure rise. Getting specific meetings on his calendar had been rough, and I'd jumped through some hoops to make sure his meetings with customers aligned with the rest of his schedule. It had been like putting together an intricate, complicated, one-thousand-piece jigsaw puzzle .

As I walked down the hall, I must have had a zombie look on my face because one of our directors, Don, stopped me in the break room and asked me what was wrong. That's all it took for me to blurt out that I had to reschedule John's entire week because he was going on travel. I told Don that it had taken blood, sweat, and tears to get many of these meetings aligned on John's calendar, and now it was all for naught.

That's when he stopped my rant to ask me an unexpected question. "Do you play baseball?"

I looked at him incredulously. Did he not hear a word I said about the calendar? I just rolled my eyes and said, "No, I don't play baseball, and what does that have to do with this anyway?"

The director calmly detailed what he was observing in this situation. "Debbie, what I see happening here is that if you were a baseball player, you'd be stepping up to the plate expecting the pitcher—who in this case is your executive, John—to pitch you a perfect, straight ball. And guess what? That's not happening here, and you're striking out a lot! Now, if you were the kind of baseball player who steps up to the plate prepared for sliders, spitballs, curveballs, and fastballs, your odds of hitting a home run would be far greater."

I contemplated this analogy as I walked back to my desk. Then it came to me. I knew exactly what he meant. I came into the office every day expecting things to go as I had planned, and when they didn't (which was almost always), I got irritated and took it personally. And it showed.

It was time for me to stop expecting the day to go my way and instead learn to go with the flow, adjust, and stay flexible.

I won't say this was easy for me to do; however, with time and a sore lip (from biting it often), I started hitting a few more home runs.

Within three years of our working together, John became executive vice president. I continued to work hard (very hard) to stay nimble and open-minded, but I had yet another lesson to learn. One day, during a particularly challenging moment, I was whining about his schedule (which I often did in those early years), and John pointed out my whining to me and told me I needed to remain calm. Calm? Are you kidding me? There are only twenty-four hours in a day, and he wanted to fill all but two of those hours! Trying to remain calm was like cramming an elephant's foot into a high-heeled shoe. John was big on not showing stress, and he expected the same from me. (There's a reason I dye my hair.)

My role was to keep everyone around me, including John, calm and upbeat whenever possible. I took his next words to heart: "Debbie, I have enough stress to manage on a daily basis. Feeling your stress increases my stress, and neither one of us needs that." Got it. In that moment, I understood exactly what he was saying. My stress was rubbing off on him. I'd had no idea that I wore my heart on my sleeve, and I needed help with this one. My job came with stress. John devised a signal, a light tap on the shoulder, for us to use if one of us began showing our stress levels. I received a lot of those taps on the shoulder through the years, and thankfully, the signal actually worked.

It was a great way to keep each other in check. I won't lie and say it was easy to remain upbeat and positive, especially on those days when I was contemplating either suicide or murder, depending on the situation or the person. One thing was certain: I had to keep my game face on no matter what or who was standing in front of me. Along the way, I learned a trick that helped. I placed a mirror next to my monitor. It wasn't to check my lipstick. I'm not that vain (although, once in a while, I found something stuck between my teeth). I used the mirror to periodically check my facial expression. No matter what I was thinking, I needed to know if I was frowning or showing anger or disappointment, or if I was smiling and looking relaxed. I often had to course correct.

Successfully developing my career at the executive level meant learning how to stay calm under pressure. I had to place my own expectations of how things should be on the back burner. Instead, my focus needed to be on meeting John's expectations, especially when his priorities shifted. It also required me to keep my own emotions in check—not an easy thing to do on certain days. How I reacted to what was happening around me inevitably affected John and other people. More often than not, people heard John and me laughing loudly and exuberantly, which always brought smiles to their faces and elevated the mood for everyone. John was instrumental in teaching me the basics of being a good executive assistant, but I had more to learn. So much more.

 MAKE THE PLAY

1. I needed to pay closer attention to sudden shifts in John's activities. In doing so, I'd be better prepared for changes that disrupted the routine.

2. I had to get control over my emotional self because my sense of frustration often showed and other people—including John—noticed and reacted to it. I kept a mirror at my desk so I could periodically check my facial expressions. That mirror kept me in check.

3. I needed to develop a mindset of adapting when things changed (and they changed constantly). Remaining flexible and shifting how I did things was the key to not just surviving, but thriving in John's world.

It was quarter-end, and our earnings results had been great. It was 2000, and Cisco had become the most valuable company in the world with a market value of $555.4 billion—an amazing accomplishment for a company worth $300 billion as recently as the previous November. John was proud of his management team and wanted to recognize them and show his appreciation for all their hard work.

One day, John handed me a long list of names. By each name, there was a note and a dollar amount indicating what the individual would get as a bonus. My first reaction was, "Is he kidding me? He's asking me to initiate all of these calls, transfer them through to him, or schedule them so he can personally congratulate each person!" I saw a long day ahead, me glued to the phone, placing calls and answering callbacks, signaling him that I had the next person on the line. I'd never seen anything like it.

John invested his time in personally thanking his teams. It was dialing for dollars all day long. Somewhere midway through placing the next call on the list, right past the G's, it dawned on me that my name was nowhere to be found. I wasn't sure of all the benchmarks that needed to be met in order to get a bonus, but I darn well knew I'd been working some long hours, and I believed I'd been productive.

As executive assistants, we should strive not to take things personally, but what the heck? How did people get on that list?

At that point, I realized that, while I was doing all the things John asked for, I wasn't sure I was taking my work beyond that level. How could I add additional value so John would see it and include me in spot bonuses?

I decided I needed some additional work in three key areas:

- Developing a deeper understanding of John's business so I could make good, effective decisions.

- Building a stronger relationship with my executive by being more empathetic and engaging in more open communication with him.

- Up-leveling my own emotional intelligence by understanding and gaining control over my triggers.

4. IT'S ALL ABOUT COMMUNICATION

I quickly became aware, as I supported John, that he built friendships with everyone he met and cultivated loyalty like no other person I'd ever known. John had so many partners, customers, and friends that I had two huge, full Rolodexes (remember those?) on my desk and soon had to get another one. John's favorite saying was: "I partner for life." I quickly learned he meant that. Our phones rang off the hook on a daily basis, not to mention the emails and mail that poured in. I was his mail room, control tower, and switchboard operator every day. So many people reaching out and so little time. My job was to scan, read, sort, and prioritize all communication coming in and keep him updated and aware.

I soon realized just how valuable this daunting task was. In sifting through hundreds of emails each day, asking questions, and reviewing the messages with John, I learned who he gave his attention to, who his friends were, and who was trying to become his friend. It was critical information. It always amused me when someone called and asked me if "Johnny" was in for a quick chat. That was definitely someone who didn't know John. He never went by Johnny, and none of his closest friends called him that. I'd reply, "I apologize, but Johnny doesn't work here any longer. If he should contact me, I'll tell him you called. By the way, who are you?"

Just like in baseball, I soon grasped who was on first, who was on second, and who was on the bench. I was drowning in information overload. It was, however, one of the most valuable and valued responsibilities I had as John's executive assistant.

Safeguarding John from the onslaught of outreach in all forms of communication is where I learned the importance of communicating with John and understanding his brand, especially after he became CEO.

I interfaced with people from every walk of life.

I picked up the phone one afternoon with my normal "John Chambers' office, I'm Debbie," to hear, "This is Tony Randall, and I'm wondering if John is in for a quick call." I smiled at that and replied with a hint of humor *"The* Tony Randall? I'm sure you are." After a few minutes and some explanations, I found out it actually was Tony Randall, the well-known actor from the popular television sitcom *The Odd Couple.* Communicating internally or externally to the world meant I had to think, react, and respond professionally no matter the person because someday, the president of the United States might just call. And guess what? He did!

MAKE THE PLAY

1. Being an effective EA meant acting as the hub for all incoming and outgoing communication. In turn, I learned the business, what the priorities were, and the who's who of who called John.

2. While I needed to protect John from the onslaught of meeting and conversation requests, I also had to remain approachable and positive in order to represent him in the best possible way. I didn't want to become an unapproachable gate-keeper.

3. I had to remain professional at all times whenever I interfaced with the world because I never knew who might call.

5. COMMUNICATION = THE WRITTEN WORD

Have you ever had to tell someone in an email that you just weren't interested? I did this on a daily basis while I worked for John. He received so many emails asking for time, money, or a combination of both, and I had to filter and sort through which ones would be put in front of John and which would be getting my infamous turndown. I say infamous because I had to learn the art of responding to emails on behalf of John by saying "no" with graciousness and tact—without ever actually saying no. You may be scratching your head and asking, "How did you do that?" It wasn't easy.

John wanted every interaction we had with people to be positive, even when that person was rude, insensitive, or pushy. Writing emails with this kind of standard became a true skill. It was easy to say "yes," but much harder to write an email to say "no" or to decline a request or an offer. Many times, John was asked to be a guest speaker, which didn't fit his area of expertise or his passion. I was the one who had to turn down those opportunities. Other times, I had to say no to good charitable organizations that reached out for funding, either from John or from the company. It became really challenging to say no when young students in college or right out of college reached out for mentoring or to request leadership interviews.

These types of requests were especially difficult to decline given John's priorities, but there was just no available time to give. I gathered some good resources that explained John's leadership style and philosophies, including an article written by *Harvard Business Review*, and in lieu of providing John's time, I often sent people some of this material so they would at least have some good information to use. I hated saying no to these young and inspiring new leaders.

Saying no in writing became an art form. If we think about an administrator's daily language, the words that continually crop up—which I call the negative words—are words and phrases such as: "I'm sorry, but I can't," and our favorite, "unfortunately." I learned that when I used any of these, especially in written communications, I gave the reader a negative experience.

Knowing John's standards for positive interactions, I developed the skill to write emails that had a positive effect on the recipient even when I said no.

I used the following process to respond to emails with requests for John or for me:

1. Read the email and be aware of my immediate reaction to it, such as frustration, anger, resentment, or apathy.

2. Write an initial reply to the email, but don't send it.

3. Review the email and try to find something positive about the person asking or within the request.

4. Rewrite the email by acknowledging their request with statements like, "I can tell how passionate you are about this," or "What an amazing event you have planned."

5. Start my response with empathy, understanding, and sincerity, which completely changed the tone.

This process wasn't easy, especially when I just wanted to say, "Hell no!" and move on. It sometimes took more than thirty minutes to craft just the right message, but it was worth it. It left people with a positive impression, like the salesperson who replied to one of my email responses, saying, "That was the nicest rejection I have ever gotten!"

Just acknowledging the person's needs and desires moved the conversation in a positive direction. Staying away from negative words and replacing them with positive words was another strategy that worked.

Making statements like "John's philanthropic funding interests align elsewhere," or "As much as John would enjoy speaking to your audience, his priorities are consuming his time right now," softened the rejection. It became a game for me in some cases to see just how positive I could make the message.

Here are a couple of examples of email requests John received, to which I replied on his behalf.

The request: *Dear John, we would like to invite you to be our keynote speaker at our upcoming gala fundraiser. We think our audience would truly appreciate hearing your views on leadership.*

My reply: *I wanted to acknowledge that your email has been received by John. He has asked that I reply on his behalf. John appreciates that you would reach out to him on a subject he is passionate about. You are right in that he receives numerous requests on a weekly basis, which of course is indicative of his leadership and team focus.*

John wanted you to know that his focus right now is working on a number of business and personal priorities which are eating up a tremendous amount of his time. He has indicated that he wants to concentrate on those priorities at this time.

He wishes you great success on your event!

....

The request: *Dear John, we are a young startup company that could really use guidance in terms of how to grow our revenue. Who better to learn from than you! Could we set up some time to meet with you?*

My reply: *Your request for my leader's insight makes perfect sense because he enjoys advising young companies in their early stages. The challenge he is faced with is that he is currently oversubscribed. John shared with me that he really wants to concentrate his time and energies on developing the new leaders on his team and, more importantly, spending more time with his family.*

This seems to be where his primary interests reside, and he appreciates your understanding.

Putting in the time to improve how I interacted and responded to people mirrored the brand that John exemplified: one of kindness, respect, and sincerity. He always stressed that we should treat people the way we would want to be treated, and that's what I did.

 MAKE THE PLAY

1. I had to put the appropriate amount of time into my written communication to create positive interactions, even when I was declining a request on behalf of John.

2. I became creative in my responses to avoid negative words and use alternative words.

3. I developed a repository of responses that could be modified based on the inquiry or request.

4. Acknowledging the other person's needs, even if they didn't line up with John's, was another way to create a considerate and professional impression while protecting John's brand.

5. Providing written resources could be useful when John had to decline requests. It was sometimes even better than offering time on John's calendar.

Many times over the course of my career at Cisco, I had to write an email back to an individual and pose as John. I considered this task an honor and a true testament to my writing abilities, but even more than that, it really made me feel like I was becoming John's business partner. No one would have ever doubted it was John who wrote those messages. It took my filtering and managing of his communications to a whole new level.

Writing as John required a tremendous knowledge of how John thought and spoke. I had to use the words and idioms he used in order for the message to come across as authentic. I started taking note of some of the words and phrases he typically used, and I saved specific sentences or paragraphs I could apply to some of my email communications. As a West Virginian, John's Southern drawl and quips and quotes were unique to him. For example, "up to my backside in alligators" meant "I'm overbooked," and "just not in my wheelhouse" meant "not my area of interest."

If for any reason I didn't know what John's reply would be, I got his views on the subject. Making mistakes when writing as John was a grave offense to him, and rightfully so. Forgetting to remove my own email signature at the bottom of the email, not changing the "from" alias to John's and instead keeping mine, or worst of the worst, keeping a thread of emails attached to the reply were major faux pas.

I made every one of these mistakes during my time working for him. Though it didn't happen often, when it did, I literally crawled under my desk. I will never forget one particular incident. John was hosting what we termed a "birthday breakfast" with approximately three hundred employees in our meeting center. It was his way of staying as close and accessible to the employees as he could by asking them to "squeeze the boss." For this activity, we used a squeeze toy created in the image of a boss.

Squeezing the boss was a chance to ask John open and candid questions. When an employee raised their hand, he would toss the toy figure at them, and they got to ask their question. When he arrived back to our office after this particular session, he gave me a grin that said: I know you're just going to love this. One of the employees had invited him to dinner, and John had said yes. I sat there in a state of shock. What a can of worms he'd just opened! Wasn't it enough that I was already constantly turning down requests from the world?

Here was one of sixty thousand employees, who had simply asked John, and John had said yes. I sighed heavily. The employee promptly emailed John to schedule the dinner. I forwarded the email to my executive administrative partner, noting that we needed this like we needed a hole in the head given how overbooked John's schedule already was. My partner, in turn, emailed me back to say it looked like we would have to bite the bullet and make it happen. I sullenly agreed. To avoid wasting any more time on this one, I immediately emailed the employee as John, noting that the employee could work with his executive assistant (me) to schedule their dinner.

It wasn't until later that day that I got a reply that knocked me off my queendom pedestal. The first few sentences said it all. *I'm excited about having dinner with you, John; however, what did you mean by "we need this like a hole in the head" and "we will have to bite the bullet" in your reply?*

In my haste to get the email out and the dinner calendared, I'd forgotten about the string (or maybe sting) of my email exchange with my team. Boy, did I learn my lesson on that one. I had to fall on my sword and call the employee to tell him what had happened. Luckily, the employee took it in stride and laughed about it, just thrilled to have his dinner scheduled.

I learned, again and again, to take my time and do it right when I wrote email responses on behalf of John. Was it hard at times? Absolutely. I was the buffer between John and the rest of the world. As daunting and sometimes exhausting as that was, I knew their positive interactions with me were how they saw John and our office.

 MAKE THE PLAY

1. I paid attention to John's language in order to effectively write for and as him.

2. I avoided knee-jerk responses (which were easy to give) to people's requests and learned to slow it down so I could respond creatively and positively.

3. I took my time so as to reduce the likelihood of disastrous errors. Once you make them, you can't take them back.

4. I had to own up to my mistakes and be accountable for my actions, both positive and negative (definitely more positive than negative).

6. COMMUNICATION = ATTENTION, PLEASE!

Communication with John was often so challenging that I had to devise certain methods just to get his attention. He ran at two hundred miles per hour every day and barely took time to sit down, much less to discuss action items with me. There are those lucky executive assistants out there who boast about having regular one-on-ones with their executives. That wasn't my story. When John walked by my desk, I felt like a poor puppy looking up with soulful, longing eyes at her master, asking him to take her for a walk—just about every day.

Because of this, I tended to let things pile up. As the pile grew, I felt heart palpitations. Like a clogged drainage pipe, the backup of paperwork, responses needed, and actions required was not pretty. During those early years, I wasn't confident enough to speak up. The last thing I wanted was to become the nagging "business wife." I don't think any executive assistant, or any spouse for that matter, enjoys taking on that role. One day, I came to the realization that this way of operating had to change. The dam was about to break, and I was going to drown.

If I couldn't get John to change, then I was going to have to change the way I pursued the information I needed to do my job effectively.

Rule #1: Have a secret strategy.

Getting the information I needed from John required me to get creative. One measure I implemented was "countertop tactics." I had a countertop attached to my cubicle wall, and that countertop was conveniently located outside John's office. I started putting nice notes from employees, articles, pictures, and other items I knew he was interested in on there. (Note: I didn't put work-related items on the counter. If he wasn't in the mood, work items would not get his attention, and getting his attention was my goal.) It didn't take long for this tactic to start working.

John would head out of his office on his way to his next destination and inevitably, he would stop by my countertop to read what was there. That gave me a window of opportunity to get answers and maybe even a signature or two. This was a way to draw him to my desk—since I couldn't sit across from him at his desk. This strategy worked beautifully and lowered my stress levels. The only problem was that other people saw how my no longer "secret" strategy worked, and they jumped on the bandwagon. They started leaving things on my countertop for John to see. The larger the pile of reading got, the less likely John was to stop by. It had to stop. So I started removing each item after the person who dropped it there departed. I put those items in what I called a "holding pattern" folder. Don't get me wrong; I absolutely made sure John saw what he needed to see. I was regulating the information flow.

Rule #2: Take advantage of any opportunity to communicate.

John called into the office often from the car. This was a blessing, but it was sometimes a curse, especially when he asked a question I couldn't answer or asked me to track someone down. Yet, there were moments when I took advantage of those calls from the car, particularly when I was having someone tracked down and we were waiting to connect him. That gave me time to talk to John. Those moments were precious.

I designated an area of my desk next to the phone as John's corner. I kept my running list of questions for him there. In that corner also sat what I called my "order pad." While I never studied shorthand, I became an amazing speedwriter. In an exchange with John, I may have only hit one item on my order pad, depending on his attention span, but having that one question answered was like being a winner on *Jeopardy*. Of course, there were always items left on the list that needed to be addressed. I give myself a lot of credit for being tenacious and persevering while maintaining calm. Sometimes the list was longer than I liked, so not letting it stress me out was an accomplishment in itself.

Rule #3: Use technology tactics.

Before texting, there was voicemail. When I used voicemail to communicate with John, the strategy was to leave him only one action item in one voicemail at a time. I figured this out because whenever I left him a string of questions, I only got a reply to the first one. Aha! Then let me just leave several voicemails with one item in each. Once he figured out my tactic, he let me know he preferred that I not send him so many voicemails at one time. (Sigh.)

To be frank, there were days when it was hard to win. Not one to be defeated, I shifted gears. I scheduled the voicemails over the course of the week. This was more effective—for a time. Then, voicemail faded away, and I was faced with a new challenge as the smartphone became the technology tool of choice and practically replaced company desk phones. It was love at first sight between John and his smartphone, and he slowly became obsessed with texting. I can't tell you how many times he showed me a text and asked me to find out who it was from. It became clear that I would need to use texting strategies to communicate, and it worked quite well once I got the hang of it. I only wish I could have scheduled the texts then (a technology that exists now but didn't when we started texting).

As John changed his communication style, I had to align my communications to what worked best for him.

Once John adapted to texting as his primary method of communication, I entered text hell. I started receiving text action items on a daily basis. Then it got scarier because John learned how to copy and paste other people's texts to him over to me to act on. I was never very

far from my smartphone, and I bet many administrative professionals out there can relate.

When emojis and GIFs arrived, I had a blast with John. One evening, he sent me a text around midnight. (He really didn't pay much
attention to time.) He needed me to schedule an important meeting. I immediately texted back a Superwoman emoji and said, "I'm
on it!" I think we both enjoyed changing the tone of our texts. Communicating effectively also meant enjoying it and bringing about a
positive response.

MAKE THE PLAY

Rule #1. Have a "secret" strategy to draw them in to you when
all else fails.

Rule #2. Take advantage anytime there's a window of opportunity for communication.

Rule #3. Use technology tactics to your benefit.

7. COMMUNICATION = DOING IT IN STYLE

Given that I interfaced with so many types of individuals, I quickly discovered that all people communicate quite differently, and I had to learn to adapt to their preferences. In fact, it was essential to my role as John's interface and liaison. Engineers prefer email. Salespeople prefer the phone. Other people prefer to use the latest technology, such as WhatsApp or Slack. And administrators? Well, they'd prefer that everyone just go away.

Instant messaging was the bane of my existence. My computer was in a constant state of "pings." I could never understand why someone would ping me with one word: Hi! And then, nothing. Or ping me and ask how I was doing. (I was in work overload.) Or worse, send me one long instant message with loads of details.

There was definitely a learning curve. Despite that, I learned to use whichever tool worked best to get results.

In today's business world, texting has slowly replaced personal interactions and other forms of communication in many situations, but texting effectively also requires skill.

I also discovered, through my own continual improvement in communicating effectively, that everyone has a preferred style of communication that works best for them. John was always direct and to the point. Our vice president of marketing was social and talkative, while our CFO was short and specific, especially with details. It became critical for me to match their preferred style if I was to exchange information. Having a tendency to want to chat or share a lot of details, I soon realized that this style wouldn't work well with those people who wanted me to just get to the point—especially John. I had to adapt. Being the communication hub for the office of the CEO required major communication skills. I adjusted my communications to suit all preferred styles, using appropriate tools to get results and forge strong relationships.

 MAKE THE PLAY

1. As the primary liaison for John's office, I had to use the methods and technologies that worked best for the person with whom I was communicating.

2. Matching the person's preferred style of communication, instead of using my own preferred method, often yielded the best results and a much better experience for me and for them.

8. STRATEGIC THINKING

One thing was certain: if I was to be successful in my role supporting John, I had better know what was going on in the company at any given time. What kinds of products did we make? I only knew the words "router" and "bridge." I thought it was pretty cool that our company logo represented the Golden Gate Bridge, but that was about the extent of my company knowledge.

I realized I needed to understand what was important to John—his priorities, objectives, and preferences. It was all I could do to keep my head above water with the day-to-day tasks that consumed my every waking moment. I had never really given any thought to the importance of raising my level of knowledge about Cisco beyond being John's executive assistant. The reality is, if I had kept that mindset, I wouldn't be writing this book now.

I thought I knew what a good executive assistant should be doing, so much so that I thought it clever to stay on top of my emails while I sat in on staff meetings. Call me blonde, but I didn't pay attention to what was being discussed. It became obvious that this wasn't such a great strategy when I got that look from John as I clicked away on the keyboard while one of the staff members went through the latest company data. It was even more embarrassing when John asked me afterward what my opinion was on the information shared in the meeting. He totally knew what he was doing when he asked me that question, and boy was I naïve. I needed to get my head up above the cube wall and start paying closer attention.

Two key events transpired during this time in my career and in Cisco's growth trajectory that got my head up from the computer and me paying closer attention. The first occurred when John decided to change the organizational structure of the engineering organization (in other companies, this would be called a department). Cisco had always maintained a central engineering organization led by a vice president or senior vice president. This was considered the company norm. One day, it all shifted. All I could think was: "If it 'ain't' broke, why try to fix it?" I had to pay closer attention to the staff meeting discussions to understand the reasoning behind this decision. It was a big change that would affect a large part of the Cisco population—maybe even me.

Cultivating curiosity became a significant component of my administrative excellence.

Consequently, once I started paying closer attention, I gained a greater understanding of John's thought process. The engineering organization was moving much too slowly to keep up with the ev-er-increasing pace of technology demands and competition. If Cisco was to catch market trends before competitors, it would require a monumental organizational shift. The strategy was to break the engineering organization into several business units focused on different products and technologies. This allowed each business unit to run at its own pace, which meant that Cisco could innovate more quickly. This was crucial in the fast-changing world of technology. This newfound knowledge allowed me to adjust the way I worked. It prepared me for the many requests for meetings that came in from engineers who were not adjusting well to the change. It also prepared me for the constant challenges of the ever-changing calendar and, of course, managing my own stress through it all.

To be clear, information wasn't handed to me. With everyone working at warp speed, I had to get proactive by being observant, noting who was going into whose offices, reading their body language, and picking up on verbal cues. I also asked lots of questions, and I had to work hard at getting over my fear of asking. Anytime I didn't understand something about our business—why the market was doing what it was doing, the next big thing the competition was planning, or why certain organizational changes occurred—I tapped into my curiosity.

Knowledge is power and opportunity. I found that understanding Cisco's business allowed me to speak about it knowledgeably and gave me more confidence in myself.

It helped me build an even better relationship with John. It also gave me more credibility with other executives who grew to trust me, rely on me, and in some cases, even allowed me to coach them on how to handle situations with John or their own administrative assistants. Many became good friends.

The second event that changed my thought process and taught me the value of learning the business occurred as a result of Cisco's first acquisition. I remember this day clearly because it was the day of our board meeting. The presence of the board members in our offices made everyone walk around on pins and needles. I was about to get my rope out to lasso John and rein him in because he was running behind schedule. The last thing I wanted was a call from our chairman of the board asking me where John was.

The John tornado came rushing into his office and grabbed his board book, a heavy monstrosity of a binder comprised of many tabbed sections with company performance indicators and revenue numbers that the legal department compiled. Thank goodness the only thing I had to manage was making sure John got his board book and signed the appropriate legal pages. He was already headed down the hall to the board room when I picked up the phone call that shook Cisco's world.

It happened to be a Cisco customer who was the CEO of a very prominent bank in New York. He was animated, excited, and anxious to talk to John. This was not a CEO I wanted to respond to by saying, "He's in a board meeting." I trusted my gut on this one. This CEO was important to John and to Cisco. Dang! So I called out to John, right before he ran out the door to the meeting, and told him who I had on the phone. He looked at his watch, a bit frustrated, and told me, "I'll call him back. I'm already running late for the board meeting."

Then he stopped, turned around, and said, "Tell the board members I'll be about five minutes late. I'm on the phone with an important customer." Now typically, John would have never made the board wait for him; however, this felt important, and I sensed it. The phone call lasted a lot longer than five minutes. I was sweating bullets after the first ten minutes passed, running to and from the board room to keep the board members updated. John was having a great conversation with the bank CEO while I was getting the dirty looks from the board.

When John finally hung up the phone, he thanked me for making sure he took that call. It seemed that the CEO was letting John know what he thought was missing in our product line and telling John what he should do to remedy the situation. Doing so could ultimately provide a new revenue stream for Cisco. John was as excited as that CEO had been. When John finally walked into the board meeting, he proposed buying an existing company that had a product that Cisco could integrate into our existing suite of products. This acquisition would ultimately solve some critical customer pain points. The board loved it. And all was forgiven.

Knowing the organization's priorities—in this case, John's customer relationships—sensing the urgent need for this CEO to talk to John beyond typical business concerns, and getting John's attention even though I knew he was going to be late for the board meeting were all pivotal to the impact of Cisco's first acquisition. Good judgment paid off for me that day.

It turned out that I was in for a really rough ride after that. I had no idea what to expect or what was expected of me. Our company had never done an acquisition before, and it was probably one of the most painful periods in my career and for Cisco. It was new territory.

 MAKE THE PLAY

1. I became curious about the overall business and started thinking beyond my daily role.

2. To face my feelings of inadequacy, I asked John and other executives questions to gain a greater understanding of what was going on both inside and outside of Cisco.

3. Many times, I relied on and trusted my gut feelings about certain situations, and almost always, my intuition was right.

4. It was critical for me to know who was important to John.

The first company Cisco acquired was Crescendo. There were as many moving parts to this acquisition as there are in a fine timepiece. All of us in the organization were on edge just trying to figure it out day to day. The skills I acquired in my early years—flexibility, adaptability, and keeping an open mind—were truly tested. Given the increase in the number of meetings he had, John's calendar became the ultimate nightmare. The meetings included finance, human resources, public relations, executive teams, employees, and of course, adding the newly acquired company's components, including their engineering, sales, and finance employees.

There were multiple board meetings, not to mention dealing with all the legal aspects of the acquisition, which required many general counsel meetings. John also had to manage his leadership team and their fears about how organizational changes might affect them. He was continually coaching Cisco management off ledges. There was skepticism in the investor world and in the press. This added even more pressure for John and for the company. There were days when I thought I was going to lose my mind and be carted off to the asylum. I discovered that to embrace this type of chaos in ever-changing scheduling, I had to take a step back and try to see the big picture.

While not always easy, asking questions and looking at the level of importance of each component of the project (in this case, the acquisition) really helped me see how things could and should fit on the calendar.

Priorities shifted constantly during this time period. I had to continually check in with John to make sure we were aligned and I was putting the right things on his calendar or removing the less critical items.

Some days the calendar seemingly changed by the hour. The acquired company's CEO wanted a meeting with John right away, or

CNBC wanted a live television interview in New York within the week, or one of John's key executives wanted to leave the company. These were all fires that needed immediate attention. Though this may be showing a bit of my age here, in those days, I used a paper calendar and 3M sticky notes for meetings because they could easily be removed or replaced as opposed to having to be erased. This meant piles of sticky notes! Being nimble, flexible, and willing to change at the drop of an "I need to schedule," "I need to cancel," or "I need to re-schedule" request helped me stay sane and operate smoothly. It also kept my stress level and blood pressure, as well as John's, in check. Thankfully, in today's business world, where Outlook and Gmail calendars are the norm, we can shift meetings in a blink of an eye.

I found myself canceling and rescheduling so often that sometimes I either forgot to put the same meeting back on the calendar or I put it on the wrong day. I noticed that many of my peers in the industry, with whom I interacted, were often in that fast-paced mode too.

It became important to over-communicate with almost a "cross-check and then cross-check again" mentality. My normal process was to confirm, via email and then verbally, the date, day of week, time, and even time zone of each meeting. I caught some real doozy mistakes that could have caused a lot of heartache. One mistake could affect so many other things, causing a domino effect, and quite honestly, I didn't want to be at the end of that chain reaction.

There were days when I was moving so fast in calendaring John's schedule that I suddenly got lost in the Outlook calendar jungle. Paper trails were often the only way I could find my way back to sanity.

I started embedding important details in John's Outlook calendar, including historical data, such as the email request; notes on why or how the meeting was requested; the points of contact and their cell phone number, photo, and bio; and any other pertinent information I believed could be useful.

Doing this not only saved my sanity, it gave me the information I needed when John suddenly asked me:

"Why am I meeting with this person?"

"How do I know this person?"

"What is the meeting about?"

"Have I met with this company before?"

John was notorious for that kind of inquiry, and I started preparing to answer as many questions as possible that I thought he might ask me. It was like being on a game show where I battled to get all the questions right. Sometimes I even had answers to questions he didn't ask, and when appropriate, I shared that information with him as well. It showed him that I was paying attention and understood the meeting request. In addition, I often offered suggestions and disclosed key tidbits of helpful information about the person or the company. I think John found this to be invaluable. It also elevated my confidence in myself and improved my business partnership with him.

I made it a point—especially when canceling a meeting—to capture the notes within the Outlook meeting and store them in a file because, inevitably, that meeting would pop up down the road as a new request. I used this tactic quite a bit in order to refresh John's memory. It was just part of my role as John's database.

MAKE THE PLAY

1. When I felt as though I was in the midst of chaos (which was most days in my career), what saved me from sinking was to remain flexible, nimble, and adaptable to the circumstances.

2. I often took a step back from the situation and brought my head up to see the bigger picture of what was going on around me, not just what was going on with me.

3. With so much happening at such a fast pace, I made it a point to over-communicate. I cross-checked and then cross-checked again to make sure I caught mistakes and didn't miss anything important.

4. Because of the state of constant change in John's schedule, I used his calendar to retain key details of rescheduled meetings by embedding important information, including why they were scheduled or being rescheduled. When a meeting was put back on the calendar, I had the historical data of who, what, why, and when to provide to John.

5. John continually peppered me with questions on any subject I put in front of him, so I prepared to answer those questions as well as questions he might not ask.

John wanted better information, not just more information, and this in itself was a challenge and an awakening for me. I had a tendency to run on and on about a particular subject, and I could see John glaze over as he lost interest. For example, if I received a call from an unhappy customer or a sales representative who wanted to put John in touch with an unhappy customer, I'd grab my pen and write down what I thought were relevant details about the situation. Then it was "game show" time as John asked me questions in rapid-fire succession about the request. I wasn't always able to answer every question, but I knew I had to try. This meant I had to change how I communicated and also create processes that captured the information John needed. Creating briefing templates allowed me the opportunity to learn what I needed to know and make sure I didn't miss any details.

Being a true business partner to John meant I needed to think as he thought.

I needed all the relevant details before I could put the information in front of John. I didn't win any popularity contests with our sales teams, and I'm sure they had other names for me besides "Queen Bee" as I bombarded them with my line of questioning along with the briefing templates. I was the pit bull they had to get around to get to John, and I developed a keen sense of smell when it came to a weak proposal. The devil is always in the details. I had to consider whether the issue could be handled by a different executive or organization. Redirecting people somewhere other than to John was a skill, and it required knowledge of the issue, awareness of who within the organization was best equipped to solve each issue, and knowledge of the business itself.

It wasn't about being a gatekeeper who never let anyone through the gates. I knew when the right person and situation should get

John's attention. My problem was that he was just so good at building relationships. Once a customer got the chance to talk to John, they were mesmerized. They no longer wanted to have conversations with anybody else in the company. He had a way of charming everyone. His favorite saying was and still is: "We partner for life!"

I think this created some angst as it became much harder for other people in the company to build relationships with our customers once those customers talked with John. As one manager shared with me one day, once the sales team gets John engaged, they're sitting in a lounge chair eating bonbons. Having John talk with the customer before anyone else just made it sweet and really easy for them, but then, the customer only wanted to talk to John. I often phrased it this way: "You're trying to put a cherry on the top of an ice cream sundae that isn't even built yet!" The foundation of customer relationships had to be built before John (the cherry) could be brought into the mix. He was just so charismatic, and everyone he engaged with wanted to deal only with him. It could get frustrating.

Don't get me wrong, John always made himself available to customers when needed; however, my role was to make sure I understood the situation and that it was handled at the right level and at the right time. I needed to gauge the level of urgency and sensitivity and the overall emotional state of the customer and, sometimes, of the sales teams. Sales account managers are often held at the mercy of their customers and the revenue the customers bring in. In response, they sometimes have what I consider knee-jerk reactions instead of really thinking through their strategy. Being a business partner to the CEO often resulted in me talking through those strategies with the sales account team to make sure it made sense that John be engaged.

Each and every time I scheduled a phone call or meeting for John, I had the requester or account manager prepare a briefing for me, detailing information on the subject of the meeting. The briefing covered a wide spectrum of information, including name, title and/or responsibility, and a photo. This was really helpful for John when he walked into an in-person meeting. Other times, it gave him a sense of who he was talking to on the phone. There were times when I had to research through LinkedIn, Google, or other sources to find out more details about the person John would be meeting with. I also included the executive assistant's name, phone number, and email, along with the information of other attendees.

There was a section in the briefing with background on any Cisco employees, which gave John an idea as to who else from his team would be joining him and why. We soon began to leave a section in the briefing for Cisco company contacts who would need to be updated with the outcome of the meeting. John tried to keep everyone in the loop and handed out appropriate actions for the team to execute on.

Within the briefing, I embedded the customer objectives, top three messages John should deliver, and any history, such as past contact. Often, John wanted to understand who the competitors were and their business revenue potential, so I included sections for that information. A photo and bio of the customer or customers finished out this section. Seating charts were an integral part of our process because John liked to know who he was in the room with. This was essential when he viewed his customer on video as virtual meetings became common. Creating, obtaining, and editing briefings became a fairly significant part of my role, and in turn, my knowledge of the business grew.

MAKE THE PLAY

1. I created processes and templates to capture all the information I knew John needed.

2. I did the necessary research to provide a variety of information that wasn't always readily available.

3. Building in processes like briefing templates allowed me to gain a deeper understanding of requests for John's time. They helped me determine priority, sense of urgency, objectives, outcomes, and whether John was actually the right person for the request.

4. I had to be sensitive to other people's needs, while still maintaining and maximizing John's time, to appropriately filter requests.

As John continued to evolve in his role as CEO, the meetings he was involved in evolved. I began to feel like a magician, creating time where there was none, pulling an elephant out from my calendar hat, and using more and more of my ESP. It became essential for me to pay very close attention to the shifts in the corporate winds. Over the course of time, John moved his focus across the company from one organizational structure to the other, including engineering, manufacturing, employee engagement, hiring (especially for key positions), and of course, sales and the customer—his true passion.

I struggled to leave behind the way I had done things. Those mechanisms I'd created, which had been successful in the past, were becoming out of date. It was time to level up once again if I wanted to be successful and win the daily game. This meant I had to align my processes and priorities with John's shifts in priorities and create new briefing documents more suited to new types of meetings. So much information, so little time. I had to get better information—not just information—in a short, summarized way. Each meeting required an entirely different set of data.

When John met with an employee who was looking to leave the company, I pulled data such as their reason for wanting to leave, their overall standing with their organization, human resources input, and the employee's incentives to stay. I had to switch gears when John was asked to meet with a skip-level employee. Skip-level meant this individual was several layers down in the organization. I had to put together information like the employee's current role, a little background on their career journey, photo, bio, and their manager's feedback. To increase ease of communication, I added the employee's manager contact details into the briefing document. I knew John would want to pass along any relevant data to them, along with the outcome of the meeting.

In the latter part of our work together, John's priorities and focus shifted once again. Just when I was beginning to feel comfortable, things started changing again. Successful high-tech companies are always reinventing themselves in order to stay ahead of rising competition, and Cisco was no exception. John used to say that a company that did not change or see the disruption occurring would eventually be left behind. Disrupt or be disrupted! Indeed, many of Cisco's competitors are no longer in existence today.

John's statement also applied to me. As change happened, I, too, had to reinvent myself. I had to change my processes, create new ones, and above all, continue to develop my people skills. The stress level was always high, so managing my personal health was also crucial.

John became keenly interested in government relationships across the globe. He was an evangelist for digitization and the effect it would have on the world. His new interest required me to pull together an entirely different set of data. The fun never stopped.

I gathered information that included everything from a country's political climate to data on the government representatives at the meeting(s), their responsibilities and titles, and the appropriate pronunciations of their names (especially in countries like India). John was a true stickler for knowing the appropriate salutation and pronouncing a name correctly. He would constantly ask me, "Is it Bill or William?" or "Jim or James?" When it came to the higher government officials, was it "His Majesty," "His Excellency," or "His Royal Highness"? If I had gotten any of these wrong, I would have felt compelled to update my résumé.

Briefings were my life. I was constantly adjusting, modifying, and adding and creating anew. But yet again, the weatherman failed to predict the next shift. There would be major winds of change headed my way as John became very interested in the innovation of startups and the startup world. This led to venture capital discussions and meetings with young CEOs (some young enough to be my kids!). There are hundreds and hundreds of startups out there and no lack of creativity and innovation. Like bees attracted to a colorful flower, our office was soon inundated with requests from leaders of these fledgling companies who wanted to meet with John. Yet again, I needed to create briefings that would capture key data for John, especially when he met these young entrepreneurs for the first time.

Given the overall craziness of the startup world (one I had no real expertise in), I needed a compass to help me navigate it. One day, I finally came out and asked John what specific areas of innovation interested him. I was drowning in the sea of innovative ideas and concepts and very enthusiastic young executives.

John wasn't interested in being an angel investor, someone who invests at the ground level to help build a company. He was more focused on startups that had at least one or two key venture capital firms already aligned with them. He was keen on companies that had a viable product that was innovative and had little to no competition.

The data I captured included things as simple as when and where these people met John. Then, I put together a snapshot of the company, which included the product, year founded, investors, press, and their top topics for the discussion with John. I often had to put on my Columbo trench coat and do additional research and investigation when some of the people who reached out were unknowns in the tech world and were just launching their startups. I checked their websites to see how informative they were about their product and to find critical details, such as who the investors in the company were (if any), who the founders or co-founders were, and how long they appeared to have been in business.

I sifted through quite a few meeting requests and eliminated quite a few more just by understanding John's focus, interests, and priorities. If those stars aligned, only then would I pitch the company to John for a meeting. I learned quite a bit about various emerging technologies, including AI (artificial intelligence), drones, and even alternate protein sources (crickets).

MAKE THE PLAY

1. I paid attention when the winds kicked up and honed my senses to notice when John began to shift his focus. This meant he was shifting his priorities.

2. Letting go of old processes that worked at one point in time was difficult. However, I tapped into my creative side to either reinvent or create new ones to stay ahead.

3. Getting better information—not just more information—for John was key to his success and mine as his business partner.

4. I had to understand what information was important to John in order to make good judgment calls in terms of how to optimize his time.

It wasn't just the number of meetings and briefings we were scheduling and producing on a daily basis that filled my days. We were also creating John's amazing yet horrific travel schedule and itineraries. These also began to change and be reinvented. John was always in the air! While flying an executive commercial may seem like a challenge at times (especially if your executive wants an aisle seat and business class), there were so many variables with a private plane option that totally created havoc in John's travel schedule. We had to consider things like runway length, pilot time constraints, and airport restrictions. (Just try flying private to India during their winter.) Who knew? On some days, I wished I could just put John on a commercial flight and be done with it.

John traveled the globe. He was out of the country a minimum of four or five times a year and out of the office almost two to three weeks per month. It was a formidable task, and it took an entire team to put it all together. The travel itinerary was an absolute work of art. Originally just a humble little Word document, it became the King Kong of itineraries. We fondly called it "The Book of John." It evolved into a table-formatted MS Word document that was shared by all who worked on it across the world. It became the standard of travel templates and underwent many revisions during planning. The pages sometimes numbered well into the thirties. There were a number of individuals who worked on the itinerary with me from the sales account teams, security teams, and ground and air teams. Collaboration at its finest.

The table format turned out to be very beneficial. Each person owned a part of the overall itinerary and, as such, only needed specific portions of it. Columns on the table could be worked on independently and then added back into the master. I had the coveted title of "Master Scheduler," a title I soon grew to dread because of the vast number of trips John took. The itinerary reflected a huge amount of data from the simplest details—time zones, weather, and dress code—to the more granular details, such as contacts, photos, titles, cell numbers, snapshots of the overall week of events, departure and arrival times, car, driver name, driver photo, and driver cell phone number. Each meeting itinerary also included locations, drive times, attendees (both customer/partner side and Cisco side), and key onsite contacts. During the planning process, we walked through the itinerary on a monthly, weekly, and in some cases, daily basis until the itinerary was as complete as it could be. I would be thoroughly exhausted and overwhelmed with the details by the time we were done. I was doing travel itineraries in my sleep.

When John traveled for government meetings, I cringed at the thought. Trying to nail down meetings with government officials in any country was like chasing the wind. Just when I thought I had it all buttoned up and scheduled with briefings ready to go, "government" happened and everything changed. Forget tying up everything in a nice neat little bow. Once again, I increased my ability to just roll with it and let things play out as they should.

Thank goodness John was comfortable with change and understood the challenges. I didn't have any control over whether a government official kept the meeting with John or not. I just had to control my own feelings about it. I did this by shifting my mindset to one of having multiple plans (A, B, and C), and keeping multiple itinerary revisions on hand. I made it a game to predict how many revisions one of these itineraries would actually have in the end. I predicted quite well, and I turned the project from nightmarish to fun. Our travel itineraries became a template that a number of other executive assistants adopted or modified for their own executives. John often told me, "I never know what I'm actually doing until I get on the plane and review the itinerary."

Supporting John was never easy because of the level of detail he required to be successful, but preparing briefings and creating and modifying templates became standard operating procedure for our office.

One shift in how I supported him occurred after we had been working together for approximately four years. I had to think differently and manage his calendar and his overall time, not just his daily meeting schedule. It became part of my normal procedure to look at John's schedule and calendar in a holistic and more strategic way. John's schedule was always packed—as most executives' schedules are. One of my favorite sayings, when I was asked to add another meeting to his already oversubscribed schedule, was: "It's like shoving an elephant's foot into a high-heeled shoe." The other saying I quoted often was: "It's like being in the control tower of Chicago O'Hare airport on a stormy day." There never seemed to be enough hours in a day to satisfy the needs of John and the rest of the world. John was the kind of executive who wanted to understand what his schedule would be for any day, week, month, or year. I became an executive assistant ballerina, as it required that I stay on my toes constantly.

I again built in procedures to keep John and me informed. For example, each evening, prior to the day's close, I looked at his schedule for the following day and provided him with a snapshot of it. I typically shared this summary with him through voicemail. The snapshot included the time his workday started, what meetings or phone calls he would have, and dress code (especially if he had a photo shoot, a press interview, or a meeting with high-level government individuals). I also included tidbits of information about the people he would be meeting, maybe a note about the meeting which highlighted the objectives and any other comments or actions he needed to be aware of.

John often shared with me that those snapshots were essential to his ability to be prepared for each day. As times and technologies changed, he stopped listening to his voicemails, which had been our primary tool of communication. This concerned me because I felt he was missing relevant pieces of data. I noticed that he was constantly texting; his smart phone was becoming his favorite communication tool. If that was the new norm for John, then it would be my new norm too. I started texting him snapshots of his day. It wasn't easy. There was definitely less data in the text than the voicemail, but he liked this method. Yeah! I took my win any way I could get it.

It was key for me to pay close attention when John's priorities changed, but I also had to be aware of the ways John shifted how he communicated. Texting him soon became my nemesis. I would have multiple texts from John where others were copied in on it too. He would text me action items, people's contact details to add into our database, and more. It was textfusion—texts and confusion. But it somehow worked for him, so I had to make it work too.

The snapshots soon took on an additional dimension. I began to see the value in giving him a broader view, such as week-at-a-glance data and monthly views in various formats, ranging from slides and pie charts to one-on-ones with calendar in hand. When the calendar got to a point of insanity, I would include quarterly snapshots of what I identified as his available hours: *Dear John, from May to July you have a total of 10 hours available for scheduling.* That got his attention. He used this data to make certain decisions. I often heard him say to people, "We're going to have to wait on that meeting for a few weeks. I'm up to my backside right now on my schedule." This always brought a smile to my face and a sense of relief. He actually paid attention. One small step for John, one huge leap for Debbie! I didn't always win, though. Sometimes, John would say, "I know I'm running pretty hard and fast, but this is one I definitely want to make happen," which meant he was listening but was still in charge.

I discovered that executives typically make decisions based on data. As John's business partner, part of my role was to do an analysis of how John was spending his time, to view his schedule in a holistic way.

In one of our rare one-on-one sessions, I shared that he was spending approximately sixty percent of his time on business operations, thirty percent with customers, and ten percent on employee and HR-related activities. He gave me a look of shock, and his reaction was immediate. "Debbie, I want to be spending more time with the customers and less time in operations right now."

I immediately started realigning his calendar based on that feedback. We broadened this process of analyzing his schedule into yearly planning meetings. We looked at where John spent his time in the previous year, what opportunities we had ahead for him to look at, and where he wanted to focus over the coming year. We even planned his personal time a year in advance. If we didn't do that, he would never have had vacation time—not good for his family life. We looked at countries and governments visited. We reviewed political landscapes, areas where Cisco could disrupt or build revenue or where we were losing revenue. When John said, "Debbie, there's a new government recently formed there, and I want to be meeting and building relationships with those individuals as early as I possibly can," it made perfect sense. Yearly planning was an unbelievable process that gave me new insight into how to be effective as his business partner. The processes I created to address his changing priorities were key. I was only able to do that by asking the right questions to understand those changes.

MAKE THE PLAY

1. I continued to improve and modify my templates as the information John required changed.

2. It was key for me to stay flexible and develop a roll-with-it attitude about things I couldn't control in order to manage the craziness of the business.

3. I decided to get more involved in John's business from a broader perspective instead of only focusing on the day-to-day tasks and events.

4. Seeing the bigger picture allowed me to provide valuable insight to John about how he was spending his time.

5. I began to do a comprehensive analysis of his schedule. This enabled me to provide relevant information, which helped John make decisions about how he was spending his time. Because he was moving so fast, he needed a clear picture of what he was doing day to day or month to month.

9. TIME IS ON YOUR SIDE. YES, IT IS!

It became no surprise to me that, as John's executive assistant, I was often overwhelmed with the workload. In fact, the better I thought I was at it, the more work ended up on my plate. John generated massive amounts of work. Picture my day as a glass bucket. It's empty. It sits on the desk and is labeled "Your Day." Soon several large paper balls end up in the bucket and it looks half full. More, smaller paper balls are dropped into the bucket, followed by other miscellaneous items like marbles and small pebbles. The bucket now looks quite full and is starting to overflow. Just how my typical day would feel. But wait, suddenly there's a cup of sand poured into the bucket, and just when I think nothing else can possibly be added, incoming skinny straws poke into all that stuff.

I was handling so many different things, from projects and travel to phone calls and scheduling, and the list never seemed to end. My favorite saying is: "If you think you see a light at the end of the tunnel, it's actually an oncoming train" because, in the administrative world, the work is never done. If I left my desk at the end of the day feeling I had completed everything, then it was time to check my temperature, for I was surely wrong.

In 1995, when John became CEO, I soon recognized that feeling overwhelmed was making me nuts and increasingly unhappy. It's tough to climb Mt. Everest every single day without at some point saying, "I'm done!" One day, I was walking down the hallway, head hung low, when one of our directors asked me if I was excited about John's new role as CEO. I just stared at him in a glazed trance. I was drowning with no life preserver in sight.

He smiled and asked me if I had ever surfed in the ocean. I promptly replied, "Absolutely not!" I am not a big fan of the ocean, especially on the West Coast where the water is cold. He then gave me a quick lesson on surfing. "First, you have to make sure you're ready for the big wave when it comes. Then, you want to make sure you're positioned to be on the top of the wave so you can ride it smoothly until it plays out. If you don't get on top of it, you'll be washed over and under as it comes crashing down." It took me a moment to contemplate the meaning of this analogy. I was going to need a surfboard, and I'd have to paddle like hell to get on top of the wave of work that was soon to come from John in his role as the new CEO. I needed to go into survivor mode.

I had to get to the bottom of this feeling of overwhelm. What was taking up space in my bucket that kept it overflowing? I decided to take a step back and document what was in my bucket. I catalogued every single thing, from answering a phone call to doing expense reports and scheduling. I simply wrote it down—nothing fancy, just a quick note here and there. After thirty days, I took a step back and looked at my list. Wow! Certain things were glaring at me. John was doing a lot of recruiting and hiring, and along with my daily duties, I was reviewing résumés and scheduling interviews for John and other members of the executive team. I was also playing host to the candidates as they came through the door. This added responsibility was consuming huge amounts of my time, leaving me scrambling by the time five o'clock came along to play catch-up on what I hadn't been able to get to that day.

I compiled the data and then looked at what I could possibly do to either reduce, mitigate, or delegate, and I determined possible solutions to my overwhelm. Holding my breath, I walked into John's office and pulled out my data to show him. He was amazed at the things I was doing and the overall workload. What was even more eye-opening for him was the amount of time it was taking to do each and every task, including support of the hiring process. John sat there for several minutes contemplating my data and my proposed solutions.

I often encourage executive assistants who become overwhelmed and feel like they're drowning in a sea of work to start this process of collecting data about where their time is spent.

It's not fun to do, as it takes more time. You have to log every little thing you do in the day and how much time it takes to do it. However, by the end of thirty days, you should have a really clear picture of where your time is going. Once you get that picture, you have to come up with possible solutions. I started looking at how this work could be handled and prepared my list of solutions to review with John.

My two possible solutions were to have human resources more proactively manage the recruiting and hiring process and remove me from the starting position and (my favorite solution) find someone who could assist me in the day-to-day business. I felt I had won the Lotto when John said, "Whatever you need to help us both be successful." That was a turning point in my support model and the start of several amazing partnerships (and friendships) with administrative assistants and executive assistants who became part of the team. This new model did come with some angst from human resources because it had never been allowed before and could eventually set a precedent for other senior executive assistants.

It started first with the impression our lobby ambassador made when customers, employees, and vendors walked into our building. Lisa was polished and professional, and her smile was energetic. That was the kind of person I wanted to work with every day. She was eager and motivated, and I loved the fact that I could mentor her. We meshed well as a team of two, and Lisa was hugely instrumental in helping me get on top of that workload wave. I felt privileged to have an administrative assistant, who was not my assistant, but my first partner and teammate. I divided our workloads, empowering her to make decisions, handle John's calendar, and take over many of those things that had been part of my daily role. This freed me up to develop new processes and work on new opportunities, and in turn, she continued to grow and develop.

A note here: John shared with me that he didn't like to have to know who had what action item or who was managing what meetings. That was constructive feedback, and I completely got it. Lisa and I had to be seamless and be seen as one fully functional team. We had to over-communicate about what each of us was working on so we could both answer any questions John might throw out at us. My motto was and has always been: "Train someone to replace you so you can go on to bigger and better things." (This is also a great insurance policy to have if you should get hit by a bus!) It wasn't easy, but it worked.

John generated so much work on a daily basis that, by the time he had been in his CEO/executive chairman role for just over six years, there were three of us supporting him. I dedicated time to training each team member in the "John" way of work, showing them what was expected based on my own experiences. Michaela was the next addition to the team after Lisa, and each of us had our own areas of responsibility. I managed John's personal affairs, as well as all government and press events, while Lisa managed John's internal company meetings and domestic travel itineraries, and Michaela handled the international travel and external meeting requests.

I picked some great partners to work with me, though I made a few mistakes along the way. In the process of building our administrative team, I learned several important things. First and foremost, I had to find someone who both John and I had good chemistry with and who we could both trust. Trust is a huge factor in any relationship, and it was imperative in ours. Second, I had to become their mentor and empower them to help me and John, not just give them the things I didn't want or like to do. Third, I had to treat them with respect. I stayed away from calling Lisa my assistant and called her my partner instead. When we became a team of three, I called us "the team." I avoided calling them "my team," which would have sent a different message. They didn't work for me; they worked with me and for John.

Lastly, I became aware that, as I mentored, developed, and empowered these assistants, they would eventually develop a desire to leave from under my wing and move on to support their own executive. (I wasn't going to be replaced as the number one EA to John unless I got hit by a bus.) As sad as it was for me to lose them to other executives, I truly wanted to see my partners become successful in their own right. I encouraged them to interview if they felt the job was right for them.

MAKE THE PLAY

1. I had to get over the feeling of being overwhelmed, so for thirty days, I wrote down everything that was eating up my time every day. This allowed me to see the big picture and identify exactly where my time was going.

2. I was able to use the data I collected to make a pitch for possible solutions to John, and as a result, I gained his support in getting help with my workload.

3. I didn't just have assistants to help me with the workload. I had true partners who helped me be the best partner for John.

4. Having partners freed me up to work on exciting new opportunities, such as training and mentoring other administrative professionals within Cisco, creating new initiatives to support the administrative community and the organization, building and leading teams to execute on those initiatives, and getting additional training for myself.

John often said, "We train the best here, Debbie, so I can see why other executives would want a shot at hiring them away."

Having a team to assist me in supporting John was a huge help in managing my daily tasks. However, my workload actually increased in new ways as demand for John's attention increased internally and externally. His travel increased, the number of meetings increased, and thus, our workloads increased. I came to the realization that I needed to be an excellent time manager if I was going to create success for myself and for John. Besides providing him with daily support, I was managing many other activities, including training and teaching Cisco employees. I had to get a handle on my own time to meet John's expectations and ever-looming deadlines.

I was at the center of our kingdom, and as a result, I was the communication hub for everyone. I was approached, pinged, emailed, and called all day long. The executive assistant lives in a world of distraction, and my world included constant texts and alerts on my smartphone. That phone never left my side even when I made a quick trip to the bathroom. This became a never-ending hill of sand to climb. Don't let anyone convince you that multitasking is how they get their work done; that's the essence of lack of focus. The brain is not wired to work that way.

At one point, I had a severe case of lack of focus, and it was killing my productivity. I sat at my desk, at the center of everything, trying to remain approachable, friendly, and aware, while inside I was stressing out about everything I wasn't getting done. There were days when I switched from one project to a calendar request to building a travel itinerary and then to an email that needed to be answered. I thought I could cover a lot of ground by doing things this way. Wrong. Instead of covering ground, I was walking in wet sand. If anything, I started making errors, like putting in wrong dates or missing bits of information altogether. I needed to get a handle on my focus.

I started by periodically putting signage on my desk to let people know I was heads-down.

I'm drowning, so unless you have a life preserver, please come back later. or *I have focusitus. Please check in with me tomorrow. I'll be better.* These signs brought a smile to the faces of people who approached me, and they often nodded their heads and let me know they would come back, call me later, or email me. It worked. I was getting some focus time back and experiencing fewer interruptions.

Using this strategy allowed me to stay focused on the task at hand and avoid distractions. I was amazed at how quickly I could get a task done when I paid strict attention to what I was doing. That's when I decided to use this method with our instant messaging tool too. Quite honestly, I never really liked the "Do Not Disturb" response that people typically used even though, at times, I was desperate for it. (And why do people still ping you even though you have on Do Not Disturb?) I didn't want to appear unapproachable, so instead, I used light-hearted humor for my greetings. This included messages like: *This better be good because my boss is reading over my shoulder,* or *Head down . . . Interruptions could be career limiting.*

I never misused the signage or messages. I just wanted to preserve my ability to focus as much as possible. Focus time allowed me to concentrate on the task at hand without any interruptions. This was especially important when I was building travel itineraries, which were so detailed they exhausted anyone who read them.

I set aggressive deadlines for myself to finish tasks like reviewing and working on emails, especially when other people needed answers and had aggressive deadlines too. My priority was getting it done! This also worked well for me when, once in a while, I put on my out-of-office email notification, letting people know I'd get back to them and when that would be. This need to focus on projects and tasks became even more critical for me as I added additional responsibilities to my plate, such as training and leading teams. These activities always took me away from my desk and my workload. I was very grateful to have partners who could step in and cover me. In fact, if I got hit by a bus (heaven forbid) any one of them could sit in my chair and keep things running seamlessly. (I was always on guard for oncoming buses!)

Given that I sat just outside John's office, there were always employees and visitors walking by to see if they could get a glimpse of John. There were days, like Take Your Children to Work Day, when the stream of employees with their children walking by was endless. I felt as if I was in a zoo and needed a sign on my desk that said, "Don't feed the animals." On certain days, signage was just not going to work to help me focus.

As John's business partner, I often felt like I was glued to my desk, my computer, and my cell phone because if I were to walk away, something might happen that I should know about. I had to break that habit asap. The only way to get certain things done was to remove myself from my desk. Letting my team know I was going to look for quiet time, I would find a place where I could relax a bit, maybe even kick off my shoes, and then focus. This not only increased my

 MAKE THE PLAY

1. I became determined to shut down the things that were distracting me from getting the most important things done. I cut down on alerts, texts, and instant messaging tools.

2. I got creative and looked for ways I could carve out focus time by using humorous signage and responses, setting out-of-office notifications, and finding a quiet place with no interruptions.

productivity, it actually felt good to be in an entirely different environment for a change.

Time management is really a lot like project management. I started to look at all of my job responsibilities and tasks in a completely different way. Each item on my list was its own individual project. All projects need a start date, estimated time to complete the project, and an ending date and time. John's travel itineraries were fondly termed my "projects from hell." As mentioned earlier, these itineraries were extensive, exhausting to put together, and required a tremendous amount of time. I would look at John's overall calendar and schedule to see what trips were coming up, and then I'd start carving out time on my own calendar to work on the itineraries.

In order to make the process even simpler, I would build out the initial travel itineraries for the year with a template that included all the necessary blanks to be filled in. As information flowed in on any given trip, I plugged it into the template. This made it so much easier for me as the trip got closer. Some days, I allotted myself a good solid hour of focus time to add details to the itinerary, and other times, I only gave myself fifteen minutes to work on it. Ultimately, I was allocating the time on my own calendar with the finish date in mind. I was far ahead of the game before John ever stepped on the plane, and my stress levels came down.

Working with my partners, we agreed to share the building of these travel schedules because none of us were big fans of the task. Though I called them works of art, the travel itineraries were detailed to the point of nausea. In some cases, we partnered on building them. Creating travel itineraries also meant multiple conference calls with various teams across the globe to walk through the schedule—another exhausting job, especially when dealing with countries in different time zones, such as India or China.

The number one tool all administrative professionals use is the calendar—theirs and their executive's—and the predominant calendaring tool is Microsoft Outlook. Not only was I using my own calendar to schedule my focus times, but I was also using it as if it were my own personal assistant. I set reminders every day for pending tasks, tasks I needed to schedule, and even reminders to breathe or take a walk. I set reminders to remind myself to remind myself! I became a reminder queen. My personal assistant (me) was so ruthless in reminding me that I had to laugh when I got irritated with myself for those reminders.

I wondered if John felt that way about me on certain days when I was constantly showing him my watch or reminding him of his next appointment. Those reminders pushed me to get things done and in a timely manner. Ten years into working at Cisco, I was not only teaching at Cisco but also at the local university, a UCSC Silicon Valley Extension campus, where we had an administrative training program, (the only administrative training program in the university environment that I know of to date). One day, an executive assistant asked me, "How do you get it all done and still teach too?" I replied, "My personal assistant, me, won't let me slack off."

MAKE THE PLAY

1. I treated the tasks I did every day as individual projects with start dates, the time needed to complete the tasks, and end dates.

2. I used my calendar as my personal assistant by adding constant reminders to finish important projects.

3. By looking at my time in a holistic way, I got more accomplished in a shorter amount of time. I got some personal time back as a result of this new approach.

One of the biggest killers of time for me, and I think for most administrative professionals, was email. It truly took over my life from the moment I got up in the morning until the wee, dark hours of night. I spent many nights, sitting in my favorite family room chair, poring over hundreds of emails that required responses or some sort of action or supplied information I needed to know. When Cisco became a global company, the email-load expanded to a nearly 24/7 responsibility. I often thought of myself as sitting on the bottom of an hourglass with sand (emails) pouring in around me and on top of me, not a pretty picture. As we all know, the more emails I sent, the more I received.

One of the best training programs I ever participated in was "Working Smart with Outlook," which gave me some basic email principles that made email hell become a manageable email heaven. If you find your stomach gets twisted into knots when you open up your inbox, let me share with you how I changed that. I looked at my emails as individual tasks that needed to be scheduled and focused. By implementing this new method of reviewing emails, I was able to review hundreds of emails and be done with them in forty-five minutes or less. This was an amazing transformation in how I managed my inbox as well as John's.

I took away from that training a simple three-step process.

STEP 1: I scanned through my inbox and looked for those annoying emails that required absolutely no action on my part and had no information I needed. (You know who you are!) I deleted those emails. During this process, I did not stop to read any other emails. (That's called distraction.)

STEP 2: I went into the inbox once again, focusing only on those emails I could answer in less than two minutes. (If you can't answer it in under two minutes, then move on!) These were the emails that really didn't require a lot of thought, such as saying, "Thanks for the details" or "Got it, appreciate it." That eliminated at least forty-five percent of my emails.

STEP 3: I read the emails that required thought and action. Replying to these emails took some time. It could be a calendaring request or an email that required research or needed a thoughtful reply that required tact and diplomacy. I made each email its own task. I won't lie to you; my task list was long, but the really cool thing about it was that each email could be scheduled to be worked on when I wanted to work it. My personal assistant (me) was now in charge of making sure I got the emails and replies completed.

As a result of using this method with my emails, I actually had less stress each morning when I opened the inbox, and I was getting things done. I was back in charge, and I had time to focus more on John's business and managing his time.

My typical day started with a strong cup of coffee and a review of my new emails, using my three-step method, and then, I scanned what I had scheduled for that day. I used my Outlook reminder system to stay focused on the tasks and actions at hand because, as all executive assistants know, we constantly face interruptions and distractions. Without those reminders, it's easy to lose track of time or what's on the list for the day. There were days when I had to schedule time to focus only on emails, especially if I had gotten behind due to meetings, travel, or special projects that consumed my time.

My rule of thumb has always been: Don't let time manage you; manage time instead.

 MAKE THE PLAY

1. I looked at my emails in a more strategic way instead of trying to answer each one as I read them.

2. Based on a workshop I had taken, I implemented the simplified 3-D method (delete, delegate to a task, do in under three minutes) to manage the incoming email.

3. I treated emails that required time and thought as individual tasks and projects.

10. DEVELOPING EXCELLENCE BY DEVELOPING MYSELF

It became quite apparent, early in my executive assistant career, that I would not survive in this role unless I embraced learning. In the startup world, I had to wear many hats, which included spearheading a project to bring in a new phone system for our offices, managing vendors, dealing with purchase orders, and in some cases, working with human resources and sales. All of these responsibilities required me to learn something new because they took me out of my comfort zone. I was determined to impress my executives and the company and do the absolute best job I could. I embraced a growth mindset to read the manual, ask a lot of questions, take some guidance, and ultimately, when all else failed, figure things out as I went.

Purchasing a new phone system for our small company was way out of my league. It required me to look at various technologies and the needs of the company, including the system's design, capacity to expand with growth, and costs. It was a full-time project. I'll admit I was scared to take this one on, but I jumped into the project to test my curiosity and patience and, above all, to learn about new technologies, how to negotiate, and how to influence the executives. The project required me to research various companies, like AT&T and Verizon, and then bring the vendors in to show me what their phone systems could do. At any given time, I had four or five phones sitting on my desk. I looked like I was in the business of selling phones myself. I created spreadsheets showing the features and benefits of each system, including maintenance requirements and the costs to expand the system as we grew. (It was like looking into a crystal ball to make a prediction of how and when we would grow as a company.)

During those months of evaluation, I learned way more than I really wanted to know about telecommunications. I put together a proposal for management based on all the data I collected (and there was more than I'd imagined there would be). The proposal included a phone system that just did the basics on up to the Cadillac of phone systems with capabilities we hadn't even thought of, such as desk alerts and paging.

Management settled on a lower-end phone system that was capable of expanding for limited growth and was within the budgeted price range. Management was happy, and once the phone system was installed, other than the learning curve, there were no complaints. In the end, I achieved the results my organization wanted. I had learned a lot, and I'd even trained myself on new parts of the business. However, I will be candid in saying I would never want to do that kind of project again. I just wanted to become more valuable to the company.

In today's business world, I often encourage other administrative professionals to seek projects outside of their comfort zone to have new experiences, learn, make themselves visible and valued, and personally develop along the way.

Working for John Chambers meant I needed to learn a lot about the business and new technologies. In the early years, I wasn't even thinking about getting training or working on my personal and professional development. I was just trying to get by and meet John's expectations. (Note: I didn't say exceed.) I'll never forget one particular day that ended up a disaster because I decided to "just wing it" with an unfamiliar technology.

John often gave PowerPoint presentations, and he often gave me hand-scribbled pieces of paper with content he wanted added to the slides. Okay, I knew how to use Microsoft Word, and I knew how to open up the basic PowerPoint template—and that was about it. (I was pretty proud of myself for knowing that.) One Friday, John wanted his presentation finished by the end of the day for a sales meeting he was attending the following week. These were the days when PowerPoint presentations were simplistic. There were no animation embeds or special effects, just plain old slides, but this was a monstrous slide deck, and John suddenly wanted to add many more slides and elements like pie charts and grids. I was winging it, trying a variety of PowerPoint tools to see how I could bring to life what he wanted. This self-taught method was costing me a huge amount of time, and my stress level climbed as the clock ticked away.

As the day went on, I wasn't just winging it. I was losing it! It was inching close to four o'clock in the afternoon, and I was only fifty percent through the deck and sweating each slide I needed to create. Then, the very thing any administrative professional dreads will happen to them happened to me. My computer froze. I stared at the screen in disbelief. I tried to save the work, but of course, with the computer frozen, that was not happening. That's when I broke down in tears and realized I was in over my head. I didn't have the skills to make this presentation great. To make matters worse, I'd made the big mistake of not saving my work as I went along.

John must have sensed something wrong or heard my sobs because he came out of his office and put a hand on my shoulder. That's when I shared with him what had happened while wiping my tears and blowing my nose. In his ever-calm and infinite wisdom, he said, "Not to worry. Let's just get one of our marketing folks, who do this all the time, to come over and recover the work." Within a matter of minutes, the marketing program manager was at my desk, reviewing what little work I had saved. With the notes for the slides, she sat down and, like the wind of a category 5 hurricane, began to re-create the slides, while I sat there helpless and diminished. It was 4:55 p.m. when she finished up the slide deck for John.

I should have gotten PowerPoint training before attempting more than the basics. Even more importantly, I should have called on experts right from the start when I discovered I was in over my head. It would have saved me a lot of stress, tears, and heartache.

In the Cisco world, technological changes in the tools we used played an important role. Just when I thought I had one of our tools down, the company would replace it with something new and supposedly improved. To me, it was new and proven painful, but I was forced to adapt to new ways of working, and my mindset shifted in terms of looking at various ways to develop my expertise. I've always been a hands-on student, so anytime Cisco offered a workshop on a new tool or application I knew I would be required to use, I signed up immediately. This became even more critical as the job became more complicated and required the use of many tools, including TelePresence, voice mobility, and internal website technology. While many of the tools and applications we used were sometimes quite frustrating, I always approached learning them with a sense of curiosity and the all-important questions: Why does it work this way, and why do we need to do it this way? I also researched various tools outside of the Cisco realm, tools that both John and I used to improve our communication and productivity in later years.

MAKE THE PLAY

1. I needed to embrace learning if I was to survive and thrive in the startup world.

2. As painful as it may have been (and still can be), I had to push myself to get out of my comfort zone.

3. To learn and further develop my capabilities, I had to jump into projects outside of my usual responsibilities.

4. As I made things happen, management was pleased that I was learning new things and becoming more valuable to my executive and my team.

5. Sometimes, I just didn't have the required expertise, so calling in experts was necessary.

The real learning began after I had been with Cisco for about ten years. I was humming along and gaining traction. Life was good until I was offered an unexpected opportunity on one of my busier days. I was head-down and focused on a travel itinerary from hell when I heard someone clear her throat. I looked up to see one of our human resources managers smiling at me. "What am I in trouble for?" I wondered. She smiled and said, "I've got something I think you'll really enjoy doing." All I could think of was the burden of adding another project to my plate. However, it would turn out to be a project that altered the course of my career.

The dotcom era was in full swing, and we were hiring employees, including administrative assistants, at an unprecedented rate. These new administrators were like deer in the headlights, just trying to navigate the constantly shifting and complicated landscape of Cisco. New employees were always steered to our Cisco homepage to find what they needed, but finding information there was like blindly walking through a maze. One link led to another, and ultimately, new employees ended up lost. I can't tell you how many calls I received from new administrators asking me how to do something because the answers weren't always on the website. The HR manager asked me if I could help these new administrators adapt to Cisco's culture by presenting a workshop HR was creating called "Cisco's Way." My first reaction was: "You have to be kidding me. I have absolutely no experience speaking in front of an audience. It terrifies me even to think about it!"

She was undeterred. "Let me get you a speaking coach. You'll be great. I know it!" Now I was the deer caught in the headlights. I had a decision to make. I definitely wanted to help the new hires, and I had the knowledge and passion to do it. I just didn't believe I would be good at it. I was scared to death when I whispered, "Okay, yes."

Over the next month, I worked with my speaking coach, who slowly pulled me (kicking and screaming) out of my shell. I received great tips and pointers to get the audience engaged and interested. At a minimum, I wanted to have fun while I was presenting and cover the core administrative traits required at Cisco, such as flexibility, creativity, and staying on top of the workload. I tapped into my creative side and came up with some props and exercises that would resonate with this group, and I practiced, and practiced, and practiced.

It was finally show time. The day I walked into the first workshop,

I thought my heart would beat out of my chest. There were twenty-five new administrative professionals sitting in the classroom, and all eyes were on me. I kept telling myself, "You're not going to faint, and you're not going to throw up. You got this!" And so it began. I shared my knowledge with them, and they ate it up.

At one point, I threw balls of all different sizes in the air for them to catch, knowing that many of the balls would be dropped. When the exercise was over, I told them, "This is what it's like here, lots of balls being thrown at you. Many, you will keep in the air, but some will drop. The key is to know where the ones you dropped went!" They got the message.

I also showed them an empty jar and asked, "What do you see?" Many of them replied, "An empty jar." I responded, "This is not an empty jar. This is a pencil holder, a flower vase, or even a piggy bank. Working at Cisco is about seeing the possibilities." Heads in the room nodded.

I even got them up and dancing. The light bulbs were going off, and they were engaged. At the end of the day, I left that classroom glowing and walking on air. Those administrative assistants were completely energized and motivated to start their new career with Cisco as they stood and clapped in appreciation. My life was forever changed that day. I had found my passion, all because I faced my fear of speaking in front of an audience, took a risk, and stepped up and out of my comfort zone.

MAKE THE PLAY

1. If I hadn't faced my fear of speaking in front of an audience, I wouldn't be where I am today in this next chapter of my life. That kind of fear keeps so many administrators stuck where they are.

2. If I was going to face this particular fear (of public speaking), I was going to need some help. Coaching was my answer, and it was a great call.

3. Stepping out of my comfort zone opened the door for me to find my passion for speaking and teaching. After that, there was no stopping me

I began to understand that, as an executive assistant who supported at the CEO level, it was important I mirror John's leadership and also represent his brand. I had to get out there on that limb, not look down, and go for it. I wasn't guaranteed any specific outcome, but I had to see what would happen. Facing my fear of speaking gave me tremendous confidence, which ultimately paid off in more ways than I could possibly have imagined.

As I grew more confident and my leadership skills emerged, I also interacted with people at all levels, externally and internally, and more specifically, with administrators in our "Cisco's Way" program. I needed additional development in my communication skills, including conflict management, teamwork, and influence. I needed a lot more finesse than I had. Time to up-level my game!

Knowing you want to up-level and develop is one thing; actually doing it is what really counts. I discovered that having a mentor and coach in my career was important because, while I sometimes thought I knew everything, I obviously didn't. I needed a guide who could direct me down the right path. Ingrid Gudenas, CEO of Effective Training Solutions, agreed to be my coach and mentor. Communication was Ingrid's thing, and I knew she could help me develop in that area. She was excited to work with me, and it was a great investment in myself to have her as my coach. Ingrid said she would stick by me, no matter how long it took, and the ROI (return on investment) would be huge. This was a personal commitment I made to myself, and it was an educational investment that paid off. (I encourage you to look into ways you can invest in your own professional development.)

I was feeling ready for our first coaching session. I was going to rock this. Just give me the workbook, and I would be off and running. So I thought. That was absolutely not what happened. Yes, there was a workbook. However, Ingrid was not only a wonderful coach; she was a drill sergeant. Each session focused on those key elements that make communication successful, starting with completely being there, in mind, body, and spirit, when communicating with another person. I couldn't move from square one without fully comprehending the exercise and passing the true communication test. Candidly, I thought I would be done in less than three weeks, but that was not the case. It took me five months, but I got it. Her coaching in effective communications was a true foundation for my communication success, then and today, with all types of personalities, including John.

Another skill I had to develop was listening. I made costly mistakes, on more than one occasion, because I did not listen. On one particular occasion, John asked me to set up a face-to-face meeting with him and several Cisco engineering team leads and the CEO of Microsoft and his engineering teams. Easy, right? Not in my wildest dreams. Getting two globally known CEOs, whose calendars were nightmares, in the same room together. Seriously? The good news was that I already knew the CEO's executive assistant quite well, and she was always a joy to work with. Together, we navigated the calendar minefield, and we finally found a date when John and his team could fly up to meet the Microsoft crew. Okay, mission impossible accomplished. I felt happy and content.

One week before John and the Cisco engineers were to fly up to Seattle, John called a strategy session in his office with the group. Within twenty minutes, he popped his head out to ask me how much time I had allocated for the Cisco/Microsoft meeting. I smiled and with confidence said two and a half hours. My confidence fell to the floor when he said, "I'm going to need a full day for this kind of meeting, so please reschedule." My heart sank. Just finding two hours had been painful enough, but to reschedule for an entire day was going to be like pulling a tooth without Novocain. That was the eye-opener. I needed to improve my listening skills. I had let my mind race off when John was asking me to plan the meeting. I'd stopped paying attention to what he was saying. I hadn't even asked any questions to get all the facts. The lesson I learned was that I should have stopped, tuned in to his directives, and asked simple questions, such as "How much time do you need?" If I had, it would have saved me from my growing migraine.

Sometimes, I had a tendency to cut John off when he was talking—jumping in with what I thought he was going to say or need. Boy, that created problems too! If I had been truly present and listening, making notes or eye contact, and staying focused on what was being said without jumping in or interrupting, I could have eliminated many frustrations and mistakes. Ingrid's communications training taught me the importance of acknowledging others, especially John. It's not something humans are naturally wired to do, but acknowledging John built a stronger relationship between us. It wasn't always easy to do, especially if I didn't agree with him, but it opened a door for better conversation. Acknowledging him let him know that I heard him. It was essential to being a good listener. Simply saying, "I understand," "Okay," "Wow," or "Got it," let John know I had heard him.

John gave me some constructive feedback one morning. "The next time I hold a board dinner," he said, "you need to make sure you're there to make sure everything runs smoothly." My mind spun, my pulse raced, and my face turned blush red. Candidly, I was thinking, "Why do I need to be there? These board members are adults, and the hostess is on top of it." Normally, that would have been my immediate response, which as you can imagine, could have started a downward spiral of defensive behavior on both our parts. Without a complaint or a discussion, I simply replied, "Okay, got it." Acknowledging John's communication helped me avoid conflicts and arguments, even in times when my thinking wasn't in line with his.

John was really good at reading expressions, especially mine, and if he saw that "Are you serious?" look, the feedback would get even more detailed. I didn't have to ask the question "Why?" because he explained that, while the hostess may be on top of things and the board members could surely find their way to the conference room, it was an opportunity to take my role as executive assistant to a higher level. John wanted the board members to have a professional, high-touch experience, but I hadn't asked what his requirements were before setting up the dinner.

My presence gave the board members a go-to person if they needed anything. No one would have to hunt down the hostess or the wait-staff should there be any special needs. From that point onward, I was always at the board dinners as the board members' personal host and guide. I got to enjoy some amazing dinners, even if I was on the outside of the boardroom door. Arguing with John would not have strengthened our relationship; however, understanding the reasoning behind his requests was a major factor in the

 MAKE THE PLAY

1. If I wanted to excel at what I did, I had to continually develop myself.

2. I discovered I was not a good listener. Changing this was a huge

factor in my success, and allowed me to avoid costly mistakes.

3. One key element of listening is asking questions.

4. Learning the very basics of communication, such as being present, listening, and acknowledging others, helped me build a stronger foundation in my relationships with John and other people.

success of our partnership.

I became hungry for more training because I saw the positive results in my relationships. For me, any training needed to also address human interactions. I was always negotiating, influencing, or managing some type of conflict in my day-to-day corporate life. I found the American Society of Administrative Professionals (ASAP) helpful in my training and development. (Find out more at www.asaporg.com.) Their PACE program is an online training portal for key administrative skills. There's quite a lot of information on this website that's absolutely free, too.

I had never really been bold about asking for funding for training, yet I knew there were a number of areas in which I wanted to continue to develop. Personally investing in myself and my training had been my m.o. for years, and while those investments absolutely paid off for me, over and over again, there came a time when I had to find my voice and ask John for funding assistance.

Our "Cisco's Way" workshop for our new administrative hires saw its numbers dwindling, and the dotcom crash completely shut it down. Cisco was eliminating jobs through layoffs, and I was losing several administrators I'd grown close to and who had been in my training classes. I was sad, and I felt lost. I was no longer in that training and teaching mode I loved when one of my peers invited me to her company to hear the founder and CEO of Office Dynamics International. This organization created Star Achievement, a training program for administrative professionals. The CEO's name was Joan Burge, and I hung on every word she said. When I discovered I could become certified to teach her programs, I was ecstatic to learn I could start training and teaching again. I accepted the invitation, but getting certified came with a price tag I knew would be hard to cover on my own.

Timing is key when you're going for an ask. I picked the right moment on a Friday when we were winding down from a successful week and John was relaxed, smiling, and joking around with our team. Once I saw the opportunity, I asked John if he had a moment to chat about something important to me. Stating it that way caught his attention. I shared with him how passionate I was about teaching, and I explained with enthusiasm that, if I could get certified to teach this particular program, I could bring a new level of thinking to our administrative community. In turn, this would increase productivity and partnership satisfaction with the management teams.

I have to say, given how excited I was, it was hard for him to say no. Because I highlighted the ROI the company would receive, he got it, and he didn't blink at the cost. I received approval, and Cisco covered the certification fee. I would be teaching Cisco's administrators once again, raising the bar on excellence. With three intense days of training with Joan and a head full of knowledge and how-to, I was officially certified.

Still, I had another fear to overcome. I was terrified to roll out the program. I kept thinking, "It's going to be hard to get this off the ground. Think of all the things I'll need to do to just roll out the first class. What if I don't do well in front of these students, and they just don't like me or the program? What if no one signs up?" It took me exactly one year to gather up enough courage to roll out the training. I had to step out of my comfort zone again. Cisco had invested in me to do this, but there I was, creating invisible barriers around me with my negative self-talk. I knew in my heart that I loved training and teaching. I looked in the mirror one morning and said to myself, "Why am I procrastinating on this? This could be my only chance to do what I love doing. Why am I scared? Just do it, girl!"

I took a deep breath and dove in. I picked a date on the calendar to kick off the class and then followed my project-based process, and with all the milestones and action items met, the class was ready. My heart was beating a thousand miles an hour as the students walked in the door. I had a full class.

I finally felt I was at home again. The learners were engaged and loving the team activities and exercises, like one of my favorites which started the entire training series and revolved around attitudes and how easily they can change in an instant. The Star Achievement program became the foundational training program for Cisco's administrators. I'm proud to say I have trained and inspired hundreds and hundreds of administrative professionals to bring excellence to their role, each and every day, for well over fifteen years. The investment Cisco made in me allowed me to pay it back and forward, getting amazing results for the company and the administrative professionals I taught.

Companies and executives who invest in their administrative professionals will find it pays off in unbelievable ways.

I've seen administrative professionals apply a new mindset to their roles; increase their awareness of their executive's priorities, goals, and visions; learn the business at a new level and increase their executive's productivity by managing their time more effectively and becoming true business partners.

One investment I had put off making in myself was going to conferences. *I don't have time!* That was my mantra for many years when I was asked if I was interested in attending an administrative conference. It was something I never thought about nor had any interest in. I just didn't see the value in attending until Joan Burge encouraged me to come to one of her conferences, which she held annually in Las Vegas. I decided to trust her judgment, given that I was already teaching her programs, so I dove in yet again.

Administrative conferences range in price from little to no cost to over $1,000 plus hotel and transportation. It can seem daunting and expensive, but I decided to invest in the conference. Before I left, I rallied my partners to make sure they'd be good in my absence, which of course, they were. I also promised I would share what I learned once I got back and that I would send one of them to the next year's conference. I was invested in their development too.

What had I been missing all those years? The conference was well attended by administrative professionals from all around the world, and the networking I did with so many people in the profession was astounding. I made many new connections and great friends along the way. I also saw the value of networking and what it brought to me and to the executive I supported. (I'll share why in the next chapter.)

The conference speakers were motivational and educational. Attending and hearing the various golden nuggets, strategies, and tips, gave me a shot in the arm. I had a renewed sense of pride in what I did, and I left with pages and pages of notes. I was excited to get back to my office and implement what I'd learned and share it with others.

From then on, I made it a professional development goal to attend one administrative conference a year and invest in myself and my growth.

I needed to get out of my daily bubble of workloads, action items, and tasks to see the bigger picture. There was a lot going on out there in the administrative and business worlds, and I learned new ways of thinking that I took back and used to make immediate changes. I also met new people from other industries and walks of life, and I got new and different perspectives on how to approach my daily tasks.

I had been head-down in my cube way too long, and my energy had gotten low. Everyone knows to charge their smartphone every day to avoid a dead battery, but I had failed to check my own battery. I needed a boost, and conferences gave it to me. I would come back from a conference and immediately (or as soon as I could get his attention) share with John a spreadsheet of all the things I'd learned and how I was going to apply them in my day-to-day activities. Not everything worked or stuck, but some things became the norm.

I don't believe human beings ever stop learning, because our brains are just wired to continually seek new information. I encourage aspiring executive assistants to continue to develop their skills to stay relevant in the business world. That's not easy to do given the pace of change, but even today, I continue to develop new skills and polish those skills that are ingrained in me. It's about growing and becoming—a continuous journey. Even after leaving Cisco and focusing on my next chapter in life, I have embraced development and learning, each and every day, through conferences, inspirational reading, and mentoring.

 MAKE THE PLAY

1. While I made a decision to personally invest in myself and my career, I had to face the fear of asking Cisco and John to invest in my development as well.

      a. I waited for the right moment to ask.

      b. I was assertive and expressed that I wanted to talk to John about something that was important to me.

      c. I was excited and shared with him how passionate I was about teaching. It was hard for him to say no to my enthusiasm!

      d. I shared how it would benefit the company by clearly stating the ROI (return on investment).

2. I got outside of my cube and attended an administrative conference.

3. I learned new ways of thinking.

      a. I grew my network, meeting many other people in our profession.

      b. I came back revitalized and motivated.

4. It was great to come back and share what I learned with my executive, my partners, and other administrators and show how I could apply what I'd learned in my day-to-day role.

Continually developing myself was and continues to be essential to being recognized and relevant in my organization. It has allowed me to thrive in more ways than I ever expected.

11. IT'S ALL ABOUT CONNECTIONS!

I f you'd asked me thirty years ago if I networked or knew anything about networking, I would have said, "Nope!" I would have thought you meant computer networking at Cisco and what our product did. I was not interested in Networking 101. John, on the other hand, was a master of networking. He was all about relationships. He was, and is to this day, well-connected throughout the industry and is the most networked guy I've ever had the pleasure to know. During the time we worked together, he attended all kinds of CEO, CIO, industry leader, and government events. Each time he came back from an event, I found a large stack of business cards laying on my desk, waiting to be logged in. Let's not forget the special notes he'd handwritten on some of them, reminders like "good guy, stay close" or "VIP." The contacts database grew into a huge, hairy monster with the tremendous amount of networking John did on a daily basis. It was one of the many reasons that communications in and out of our office were constant, and that networking and the always-growing database paid off for me.

The benefits of John's networking were noticeable. He stayed tuned in and on top of tons of relevant information because of his personal network. Seeing this, I started thinking maybe Networking 101 wasn't such a bad idea for me.

If you don't have a network, you have to start a network, and so I did.

I decided to bring all thirteen of Cisco's executive assistants together for the first time with an email invitation to meet in the boardroom. There we all were, sitting around our company's board table for our first meeting, looking at each other with question marks in our eyes. None of us knew each other well (other than through email or over the phone), and it was great to see them recognizing each other almost for the first time.

"Together, we have the power to make great things happen that will benefit our organizations and our company," I said. "Let's put our heads together and create it!" We became a network, and it was a powerful one in terms of the information we shared and the benefits the company derived from it. Healthy networks grow, and this one definitely did. Our original group of thirteen members expanded as other executive assistants joined Cisco. Our focus shifted to key programs that would assist the company, our own organizations, and our administrative community. Brainstorming created an amazing effect on the group as everyone got to know each other, and we just couldn't help but share ideas, important news on the latest technologies, and best practices. By creating this network, we all were in the know, informed, and building strong relationships.

Thriving networks create other networks, like a vine, ever-reaching, spreading, and climbing. Executive assistants formed their own networks within the company. They created committees, such as Rewards & Recognition, Mentoring, All Hands Administrative Meeting, and Administrative Learning and Development. Getting to know many of the committee members gave me great insight into some skills and knowledge I didn't have. Knowing the strengths and talents of many of those administrative professionals allowed me to create a support hotline (and believe me, I definitely needed it sometimes).

This was a unique time in my career because, in branching out and co-leading, I was building yet another, broader network for myself. I have always strongly encouraged other administrative professionals to step away from the day-to-day role and play a bigger part in the administrative community, and in turn, grow their network. Networking is about joining a team, being a part of something, and reaping amazing knowledge and opportunities. I've also encouraged executives to give their administrative professionals the time and opportunity to be part of a team. It can become a pipeline of ideas and information that could be important to the executives and the organization. I often shared with John some of the new ideas our team came up with that could potentially solve a problem or information about what some of the other organizations were working on.

My connections were robust, but I didn't stop there. Soon after John was promoted to CEO, I learned that the scope of my role had just grown exponentially. One frantically crazy day, I answered the phone with an exasperated sigh as the woman on the other end of the line introduced herself to me. I was thinking, "Oh no, another sales call, somebody wanting something from John." She began to explain herself, and I stopped looking at the computer to listen. She was supporting a CEO, just as I was, and she was contemplating putting together a group of like-minded executive assistants who supported CEOs in Silicon Valley. Would I be interested in joining it? All I could think of was how much time this would take out of my already fully loaded days.

What she said next actually swayed me. Given our roles working at the CEO level, there was really no outlet for sharing our challenges, issues, or best practices. I had to admit this was true for me. I said yes, and my network expanded once again. The group became the Silicon Valley Catalysts Association (SVCA), an organization of twenty-five EAs supporting CEOs in Silicon Valley. This network of women and men provided great ideas and best practices that I could use. Topics that were hugely valuable to me included ways to manage our stress (a common challenge at the CEO level), how to communicate in a multigenerational organization, and how to update and boost our LinkedIn profiles. I was connecting with the executive assistants of the CEOs with whom John was connecting. It was pretty cool.

Connecting with your peers can make magic happen because it's not always what you know that gets things done. Sometimes, it's who you know.

Here's one of the great stories I like to tell about the power of the network. I was hardly ever out of the office unless I was training or on vacation. Working for John was often a ten-to twelve-hour day. It felt like I had five china plates on poles, spinning in the air, and I was hoping one wouldn't drop. It could be exhausting. Even setting boundaries, such as leaving early for a weekly Jazzercise class or not reading my emails on weekends (unless it was urgent), didn't always work. It was mid-December, and I was laying low on my trusty couch with a nightmare of a head cold, missing yet another day of work, something I rarely did. I had my trusty laptop on my lap as I tried to catch up on emails flooding in, feeling sicker because of it, when my cell phone rang. It was my executive assistant partner calling, and I thought, "How sweet to call and check up on me."

Nothing could have been further from the truth. She was a bit panicked and asked me if I had secured tickets John had request-ed for a particular conference. My head cold became a panic attack. What tickets? What conference? I was reeling. This was not only a premier event, but it also usually sold out six months in advance, and apparently, I was supposed to have gotten tickets for John. I was nauseous at the thought. How could I have forgotten? Did he even mention this to me? My mind bounced around like a pinball, but whether John had forgotten to tell me or I had forgotten didn't matter. He was expecting tickets. I was in a pickle, and I knew it. The conference was only four months away.

As I sat there, wrapped in my blanket, my mind raced. I looked up the conference online. I saw the list of "who's who" attendees and a notice that the conference was already sold out. These were not tickets you could get on Ticketmaster or StubHub. It was time to either write up my resignation or pull out my Superwoman cape from wherever I had stashed it and put it on.

Suddenly, like a bolt out of the sky and into my brain, I remembered the last SVCA meeting I attended. One of our members had mentioned that her executive had a contact who was well connected regarding hard-to-get tickets. Scrambling off the couch, blanket flying, I grabbed my notebook and searched for the name. I finally found it. (I believe the higher-ups were smiling down on me that day.) I called the contact, and once I described my issue, he completely understood and said he would get to work on it. Relief was just a Tylenol cold tablet away. Then he casually asked, "Oh, by the way, did you book transportation or hotel rooms? Those are probably going to all be booked too." I meekly replied, "No, I didn't even know until today that I needed the tickets."

I sweated out my cold over the next couple of days, waiting for him to get back to me. He finally did, and it was the cure I needed. He'd obtained the tickets and secured a suite and transportation. I did a happy dance and virtually hugged him at the same time. While I have to say it was a tense few days of waiting, it worked out for John and for me, and John was happy that I'd made the miracle happen—even though, for him, it was just another job well done.

MAKE THE PLAY

1. As the hub of information flow for my executive, who I knew was just as important as what I knew, so growing my network inside and outside of the company really helped.

2. In growing my network, I created an amazing pipeline of ideas and information that would be important to John and to me.

3. Executives can gain insights and information and see impossible things happen for them just by recognizing the value and power of their executive assistant's network.

12. LEAD OR BE LED: A CHOICE

I was pretty much a wallflower in my early days as an executive assistant. I definitely lacked the confidence of my seasoned counterparts, and I didn't consider myself a leader. I followed. Quite honestly, I was scared of stepping up to the plate, making myself more visible and vulnerable. I soon discovered that, as I took baby steps onto the playing field, the fear subsided and my leadership skills slowly emerged.

As I worked with John every day and observed his interactions with people, I learned the secrets of true leadership. I became a student in the John Chambers Leadership Program. The first thing I discovered about John's leadership style was that he had a unique way of opening himself up to people, putting them at ease, and sharing a bit of himself with them. Being a leader like John meant I had to be willing to open myself up to others. This required being vulnerable—what a tough thing to do. Suddenly everyone sees you differently. I wanted them to see me as human with human frailties, someone who made mistakes, and someone who they could approach, who cared and was open and friendly and fun. Not someone who felt they were above everyone else. (When people see you that way, they won't tell you when you have a bit of spinach between your teeth.) John did it every day. So would I.

Leadership also meant caring. Here was a CEO, one of the busiest people on the planet, with a non-stop schedule that exceeded twelve-hour days, and yet, he would stop the clock to talk to an employee in need, a customer in a panic, or an old friend from the past. This made him the master of long-lasting relationships. By the way, John behaved this way with everyone, from the top executive management to the ranks of the janitorial staff—valet attendants, waiters, and hotel staff included.

Caring was a leadership trait I had to really work on. It pulled at my heartstrings when employees reached out because they had lost a family member or were dealing with illness. I was their bridge to communicate their needs and issues to John. On the other hand, caring was also a leadership trait that could make me absolutely nuts. It's hard to stop everything you're in the middle of, especially if you're under an aggressive deadline or running late for a meeting, to listen and empathize or take some action when someone needs you. It takes practice. Believe me, there were days when I wanted to block the request or the outreach to John or ignore the email or phone call to me from someone who needed one or both of us. But people responded to the thoughtful attention. They admired and respected how John and I treated them.

Being somewhat introverted and closed, I wasn't easy to get to know. In fact, many administrators who didn't know me were somewhat intimidated by me. I had never been one to reach out, but it was time for me to step it up and lower my executive assistant walls. (This was before we had collaborative workspace environments.) People tend to respect leaders who understand them and care about them and, as a result, are willing to support those leaders in the toughest of times.

John is truly a visionary in whatever he focuses on, and this was yet another leadership trait that I grew to admire. (I don't know if all administrative professionals I come in contact with feel they are visionary.) Visionaries see the world in a way that's creative, innovative, and solves problems. Many APs and EAs have this quality, whether they know it or not, and I decided to tap into my own.

I got a huge boost in this area when I decided to teach within Cisco. I was interacting with administrative professionals and executive assistants from an entirely different level and perspective. I wasn't in the classroom as the EA to the CEO. I was their teacher.

Over the tenure of our partnership, I watched John continually take risks in everything from mergers and acquisitions to creating new products and guiding employees to go in new directions. He was actually teaching employees how to become leaders themselves. I was very fortunate to learn from him, and in doing so, I discovered how to become a leader. I took a huge risk when I decided to teach for the first time. I wasn't confident or comfortable standing in front of groups or being bold in my actions. However, I had been strongly encouraged by HR to share my knowledge about Cisco's culture with newly hired administrative professionals. When I was offered the opportunity, I had a choice. I could say no, and they would move on to find someone else who might be able to do it; or I could say yes and possibly help these newbies adapt quickly and as smoothly as possible to the craziness of the company's culture, something I had lived and breathed at the top for more than ten years at that time. I made my choice. I stepped out of my comfort zone and decided to try something new. Leaders take risks without knowing what the outcome may be.

I realized, soon after I started teaching, that I had a gift for inspiring these administrators to become so much more than they gave themselves credit for or believed they could be. One executive assistant who I coached was initially terrified of speaking in front of a group, but she actually stepped on the stage at an All Hands Administrators Meeting and gave a presentation with confidence. It reaffirmed that my gift was paying off for others. I loved watching her shine.

One element of leadership already inherent in me was curiosity. I asked a lot of questions of my peers, management, and John when I met with an issue that baffled me. Curiosity leads to problem-solving, and as John's executive assistant, that's what I soon found myself doing—and loving it. Any great executive assistant will tell you problem-solving is almost second nature because they're faced with challenges every day, from a simple calendar mistake to travel plans gone wrong. Executives need an executive assistant who has a problem-solving mindset. Problem-solvers not only make things better, they come up with innovative solutions that ultimately save time and money and increase productivity.

Over the course of my career in supporting John, my leadership ability—which had been hiding inside of me for a very long time—slowly emerged. It grew exponentially as my interaction with the administrative community increased and as I watched John in his day-to-day interactions. My love for the administrative role and for those administrative professionals who worked alongside me at Cisco became more important to me. As a result, with creativity kicking in, I became proactive, jumping in when I saw an unfilled need.

Executive assistants who exhibit proactive behavior and take initiative are truly leading the way.

In my years working in the Cisco culture, there were often things that the company did or didn't do that set me on a path of creation or problem-solving. For instance, at one point, our administrative community needed a shot in the arm. Everyone had been dealing with organizational restructures and layoffs, and they had their heads down, managing change with little reward or acknowledgment. I got proactive and was determined to create an initiative and a team focused on bringing a new program to life.

Our very first recognition program was the "Bravo Award," and it was well received by the administrators. This was an annual recognition of an administrator who went above and beyond her role, someone who exhibited leadership, creativity, and a strong work ethic. It was a nomination by peers and managers, and we recognized this administrator at our annual All Hands Administrators Meeting. It was a huge deal to be recognized by the company, and even John would acknowledge the winner with a letter sharing how proud he was of this person. The Rewards & Recognition program really put a focus on what our administrative community needed, to be valued and recognized for the hard work they did.

Leading that program was reward in itself for me, but leaders don't just stop at one win, so I started looking at other areas where I could proactively put my energy. Focusing on the administrative community was like having a blank canvas to paint on as I saw so many areas we could concentrate on that would ultimately pay off for Cisco and the administrative community. For example, I saw how frustrated our CFO got with some of our employees who took advantage of Cisco's money, taking home office supplies, fudging offsite expenses, and purchasing items that were probably not necessary. In response, I created, along with other great like-minded administrators, the Frugality team.

Our charter was to put frugality back into our company's day-to-day operations and into the employees' mindsets. Sadly, as the company grew, the team found it harder and harder to hold on to the initiative as new technologies and processes were put into place. That didn't stop me. I created an initiative called the Resource Task Force (RTF) to solve the problem of losing the intellectual capital in good executive assistants when downsizing put them at risk of losing their roles when their executives departed the company. My idea was to take those exceptional executive assistants and administrative professionals (our intellectual capital) who were at risk of losing their jobs and instead of letting them go, retain them within the company and have them support executives who were without their own support. This was an exceptionally good model to fill in for executive assistants who were out on maternity leave or on vacation. It was similar to an in-house contractor service.

The initiative had several flaws that I didn't initially foresee and which ultimately caused a slow and painful death for the RTF. These included oversights like not having anyone dedicated to managing these EAs and not designating a place for their headcount in the budget. It was a great idea, but it was like pushing an elephant up a steep hill, so it just never took off. But I didn't give up.

Great leaders will sometimes have what they consider magnificent ideas which ultimately fail. The key is to not despair or give up but to keep going, modify if needed, or just change directions.

I noted that John had to do this on occasion, and so did I. What I truly loved about Cisco's culture was that the employees, and specifically the administrative community, embraced leadership when it came to solving problems creatively. When one thing didn't work, I would just move on to the next big idea.

As the chief executive assistant and a person who was always creating, I seized opportunities wherever I saw a need in our administrative community. It also helped that I was empowered by John, who supported my efforts. I considered our administrators to be Cisco's power source for making amazing things happen. Big ideas came in the development of initiatives like the Mentoring Team, which helped administrative professionals and newly promoted executive assistants get training and guidance on how to be successful in the company. The Administrative Learning & Development team (ALD) was formed to provide additional development and training for the administrative community, as was the committee known initially as All Hands Administrators Meeting, which morphed into Administrators Learning Forum (ALF), and is today known as Administrators Professional Summit (APS).

One of the most endearing initiatives I helped create was Global Remote Administrators Connecting Effectively (G.R.A.CE.). This idea was sparked when I attended the Office Dynamics Administrative Conference and connected with one of Cisco's remote administrators who was attending on her own from the East Coast. She came up to me after one of the sessions to share with me that she was excited and glad she had made the trip. She said the conference was hugely worthwhile, and she wished other remote-side administrators could have joined her.

That started a conversation between her and me about the need for remote administrators to feel connected to each other and to the corporate offices. Remote administrators typically work alone in their home offices and can often feel out of the loop. Thus, a brand new initiative was born, one that's still going strong with twenty-five-plus remote administrative members. They come together with quarterly conference calls to share best practices, learn new things, and feel connected beyond the home office.

These initiatives truly set Cisco apart from any other company in the world. No other company focused on its administrative community the way we did. Our administrators were some of the best-trained people in the valley, and other companies wanted to hire them.

I believe executives should seek out business partners (executive assistants) who are leaders in their own organizations. These executive assistants take initiative and creatively solve problems, all while remaining humble, caring, and compassionate with their peers and those administrators who look up to them. They lead teams and bring solutions to the table that will ultimately provide true value to the companies and executives they support.

 MAKE THE PLAY

1. Becoming a leader meant I needed to start by taking baby steps onto the playing field to get past my fear and slowly watch my leadership skills emerge.

2. Working with John every day and observing his interactions with people, I learned the secrets of true leadership and compiled them in the leadership checklist.

LEADERSHIP CHECKLIST

- ☐ Open up and become vulnerable.

- ☐ Be caring, compassionate, and empathetic.

- ☐ Seek to understand.

- ☐ Be assertive when needed but never aggressive.

- ☐ See the world in an entirely different way, solving problems and being creative and innovative.

- ☐ Take risks without knowing the outcome.

- ☐ Have a strong sense of curiosity, which leads to problem-solving, which in turn leads to saving time and money and increasing productivity.

- ☐ Be proactive.

- ☐ Don't stop at one win or success. Keep going.

- ☐ Know that sometimes what seems like a great idea may fail. Don't give up. Just change direction.

- ☐ Practice becoming a leader who others respect.

13. EMOTIONAL OR EMOTIONAL INTELLIGENCE?

One of the top soft skills an executive assistant should have in her career bag is the ability to communicate not just effectively, but exceptionally. This isn't a skill we're born with. It's a skill we must cultivate and continue to develop. It was a skill I had to learn, especially after John was promoted to CEO. This skill includes the ability to become aware of and manage the messages we communicate through our emotions, our body language, and the words we use. This is called emotional intelligence.

In the early years of my career, I was one of those people who wore her heart on her sleeve. You knew by looking at me what I was thinking and feeling. Supporting John was a very stressful role, and I interacted with a vast number of executives, board members, and administrative professionals within the organization. I had to filter many requests for John and for me on a daily basis, and stress became the new norm for me. You could read it when I was angry. You could see it when I walked down the hall, shoulders slouched and a frown on my face. Believe me, I didn't hold back when I felt agitated.

One day, John was doing a number of interviews to look for a new member for his leadership staff. I was handling the candidates and the interview process for him, which included lining up members of John's existing staff to interview these candidates. It was time-consuming. I had to work with the candidate's schedule, John's schedule, and other executives' schedules, and it was like trying to put together a thousand-piece jigsaw puzzle. I finally had the stars aligned and everyone in place for the candidate to meet with, and I was ready to head to the lobby to get the candidate for his first interview with our vice president of sales.

Before I even had a chance to leave my cube, the executive assistant for the VP of sales phoned me to tell me her executive was now unavailable to meet the candidate. I felt the heat rise on my face. I was furious. I had worked really hard to get this interview schedule lined up, and the VP of sales was key to the process and also was scheduled to do the first interview of the day. I stomped into the executive assistant's cube down the hall and started a tirade of accusations, complaints, and demands. "How could you cancel this interview? Don't you understand how important this is to John? Now I have to babysit this person until his next interview, and what am I going to do with him until then? I suggest you either change your executive's schedule or find someone to replace your executive for this interview right now!"

I stormed back to my cube to pick up the paperwork and greet the candidate. I was certainly not in any mood to be cheery and welcoming to this poor person waiting in the lobby to be escorted upstairs. Adjusting my attitude, I managed to welcome the candidate and explain the situation to him. He was very understanding, and I placed him in a quiet conference room with some reading material and coffee and told him I would be back shortly to get him started on his interview schedule.

As I walked back to my cube and past the cube of the executive assistant for our VP of sales, I heard sobbing. I looked in and saw her wiping her eyes with a tissue. Here was a young woman I'd yelled at minutes earlier, who was obviously upset by my behavior. It's a moment I will never forget. I realized that, whether I worked for the CEO or not, I didn't have the right to yell at or degrade anyone else just because my interview schedule was messed up. I felt horrible for what I had done and walked over to her, put my hand on her shoulder, and apologized for the way I had acted. She accepted my apology, and as people are wont to do, told me how I had made her feel.

As executive assistants with so much on our plates, being stressed is definitely the norm, but exceptional executive assistants are keenly aware of their emotions and use tools to manage them. Controlling our emotions is especially necessary in the most frustrating times, like when other people just get on our nerves (and boy, they will definitely do that to us). The higher an executive assistant gets in the organization, the more challenging it becomes to keep negative emotions in check. We're interfacing at a highly political level with other executives and board members who, due to the nature of their roles, can be very demanding, sometimes to the point of ridiculousness.

As time went on, I learned how to quickly recognize that I was getting to my boiling point. When this occurred, I used different tools to calm down.

Sometimes, I got up and took a walk. Getting away from my desk was a rare thing, but I knew that escaping the source of frustration was healthy. On other occasions, I stopped what I was doing and engaged in some internet surfing, maybe looked for a brand new pair of shoes, finally read an article I had saved, or checked out the latest web training available. Doing any of these things allowed my mind to calm down, focus on something else, and put my emotions back in check.

Communication became far more complicated for me as John's chief executive assistant. I was interfacing with what felt like the entire organization and especially with many administrative professionals at all levels. I soon realized I needed additional development in how I was communicating, as I strongly feel every one of us does. That was when I decided to reach out to my longtime friend and mentor, Ingrid Gudenas of Effective Training Solutions. I set up a dinner date with her, and over the course of our conversation, I told her I really wanted to step up my communication game. I felt I was adequate in my communication skills, but I wanted to represent John and the office of the Chairman and CEO in the best possible light.

There were certain people who caused me stress and irritated me, and I didn't want to fall into negative communications (as much as I was sometimes tempted to). Ingrid shared that she had just the program for me, and I was ready and eager to sign up and start. Candidly, I thought this would be a piece of cake. Give me a workbook, instructions, and training, and I would be great!

I was completely wrong about this program. Ingrid started our first night by teaching me what it means to be present as the baseline for communication. This was probably one of the most difficult exercises I ever had to complete, and it took me several sessions to get it. Being present requires you to be in the moment, completely undistracted, with a clear mind. I realized that this was something executive assistants are constantly challenged with because of the constant interruptions we face in our roles. I tended to have a constant stream of people walking by my cube in front of John's office, many stopping to say hi or checking to see if John was in. Being present was hard and more so when I was working on a project, creating a travel itinerary, or composing an email and had to stop what I was doing to acknowledge someone standing at my desk.

The other area I discovered I needed to develop was my ability to fully listen to the other person.

Active listening is a part of emotional intelligence. It allows you to empathize with people better and creates a connection that develops when people feel heard and understood.

It's one thing to learn to be present when someone comes up to you, but to truly listen and focus on what they're saying is also challenging. I'd be thinking of a million things I needed to be doing while someone was talking to me. This was one of my biggest weaknesses in my early years of working with John. He would start out sharing some detail with me, and in my mind, I was already planning out the next steps I needed to take without listening to everything he had to say.

One incident really opened my eyes to how little I listened. John, every year for a number of years, traveled to the East Coast to attend the Final Four basketball games, where the top college teams competed until there was a champion. Each year, John and his wife took one particular couple with them, and I arranged all the logistics, such as hotel and transportation. One day, John mentioned to me that he was definitely interested in going again, and before he could fill in the blanks for me, I was already on the phone making the necessary arrangements for him and the other couple. The tickets to the Final Four are very expensive and difficult to get, so I wanted to get on top of it as quickly as I could.

A few weeks later, John and I were having our one-on-one time together, and he asked about the Final Four. I was quite proud of myself when I told him I had secured the four tickets, hotel, and transportation and had already been in contact with the other couple. He stared at me with a surprised, almost frustrated look—not the look I was expecting. When I asked him if I had done something wrong, he explained that he was actually planning to bring a different couple this year and thought he had indicated that to me in our conversation.

I was aghast. I attributed this error to not being present or listening fully to his instructions. John decided to move forward and invite the other couple anyway, which added additional costs for him. I felt absolutely horrible—lesson learned. Moving forward, I would always stop what I was doing when John was talking to me or providing instructions and fully focus and listen to what he was saying (not always easy, by the way, given John's southern drawl and fast way of talking—try transcribing his notes!). I also noticed that, over time, I developed a bad habit of jumping in when he was providing details, almost assuming I could answer the next question or know the next word before he could finish. John had a sweet, but subtle way of reminding me he wasn't finished talking. Boy, did I have a hard time with that for many years, as John could probably attest.

As John's executive assistant and business partner, I learned the value of truly being present and listening and what could happen if I didn't. This paid off for me with the rest of the organization and the many administrators I interfaced with on a day-to-day basis. Whenever someone came to my desk, I would stop, focus on the person talking, and be present. I learned so much more about the people who worked with John and the company, and I captured details that might have otherwise been missed or ignored, all valuable intel to John and myself in terms of keeping our fingers on the pulse. I'm sure people also left our conversations feeling more heard and understood than they otherwise would have.

The "being present" and listening skills I honed and polished set me apart from other executive assistants and truly made me John's business partner.

It was harder when I was on a phone call or in a video conference meeting, so in many cases, I had people repeat themselves to make sure I'd heard them correctly. As executive assistants, these modes of communication are far more challenging for us because of distractions that naturally occur every day in our jobs. I found that, in some cases, I just needed to leave my desk to find a quiet place where I could focus and be present, to be part of the call or meeting.

In continually developing my communication skills, which included speaking in front of audiences and teaching, I felt my overall level of confidence go up. In my early years as an executive assistant, I was confident in how I did my job but not in who I was. There I was, with only a high school diploma, working with so many highly intelligent, high-level executives, graduates from Harvard, Yale, and Princeton, among other prestigious schools. I can honestly say I felt a bit inferior amongst them, and John was one of those people. I looked up to him, as I still do today, because he was and is such a visionary and so smart in my eyes.

I would sometimes lose my nerve when asking John a question or telling him something, thinking he might see it as dumb. As a result, I found myself having a few blonde moments in his presence. For instance, I was planning his annual leadership offsite in Alaska and coordinating a number of people from across the country. Several of his key executives had to fly into Alaska via commercial air, and the plan was that John's personal plane would then transport them to the lodge from there. One group wasn't going to arrive in Anchorage until almost midnight. When I shared my concern with John about the late arrival and suggested they overnight there and depart the next morning, John got this funny look on his face.

"Debbie, it should be no problem for my plane to pick them up," he said. I promptly replied, "John, it will be after midnight, and it will be dark." John said, "Debbie, the plane has lights." A blonde moment! Not to mention that in Alaska, it really doesn't get dark during that time of the year. There were definitely a few more moments like that when I just had to laugh at myself and not take things so seriously. It was sometimes better to make fun of myself than to cry or take offense. In doing so, I learned, had fun, and was able to just be human.

Slowly, and with continued focus on my communication skills, I grew out of that feeling of inferiority. In the latter years of my career, I became bolder about asking John questions or making statements, even when it might be political or personal. He was always direct with me, as I learned to be with him. This confidence is what I believe gave me a seat at the table and put me in a leadership position with the administrative community and the executive community. I spoke up when I felt it was necessary, especially as it related to suggesting change or trying to solve a problem. When I was on teams, I felt confident enough to share bold ideas, knowing they might get shot down. I was also able to calm growing tensions or change the course of the conversation.

I gave myself the title of chief executive assistant when John became CEO in 1995, having heard a peer of mine give herself that title. It made sense, given there was only one executive assistant working at that level in the company, and that was me. When I asked John if I could change my title, he gave me the biggest grin and said, "Absolutely, but it doesn't come with a raise," and I accepted that. Since then, several of my peers have adopted this title too.

That being said, even as chief executive assistant, I often had a target on my back because not everyone liked me. Hard to believe, I know, but when you grow into a position of empowerment and power, some people question how you got there and some are envious. I just didn't let it affect me. If I had, it would have shown, and I didn't want that. To be a powerful leader, you just can't let them see you sweat, especially over whether people like you or not. I cared more about being professional and doing what was right for the business.

I have always focused on communication and the ability to do it effectively, even with those people who are difficult to communicate with, and I attribute that ability to my years of developing those skills. On more than one occasion in my career, I ran into situations that required every ounce of those skills. Having the confidence to manage conflict was essential in my role. Conflict management also required empathy and judiciousness, traits of emotional intelligence. For example, one of my administrative partners (of several that I worked with), Jenny, was brilliant on many levels and changed some of the processes we used in our office, making them more effective. I am a creature of habit, but I always welcomed other members of the team to bring in new ideas and ways of doing things. It's something leaders need and should require.

What became apparent, however, was that Jenny was rubbing members of the broader team the wrong way. Relationships were becoming strained, and several team members shared their frustrations with me. Jenny questioned everyone about everything. It was clear that I would need to step up to speak to her about it after the complaints became numerous. I never found it easy to have these kinds of conversations, but I learned that, unless you face the issue head on, it will fester and create more anxiety and stress, which the team and I did not need. I had my script prepared and specific examples I wanted to share with her. I can remember our conversation as if it were yesterday.

I started out by sharing with her how impressed I was with her abilities to look at things from a different angle and make improvements to our team processes. However, I explained, questioning others on the team about how they did their jobs created angst, something our team couldn't afford. When she realized I was actually providing constructive feedback, two things occurred. At first, she became defensive, a position I've taken myself in conversations when I received feedback from John. Second, a tear formed, and I could see she hadn't realized the negative effect she was having on people around her.

I gave her some specific situations in which her questioning of others wasn't appreciated. She replied, "I'm just trying to understand the how and why of what they're doing," and I told her, "I appreciate that, but it's probably the way you're approaching them and your tone that people have a problem with." Together, we came to the conclusion that her mind was wired to constantly seek to improve things, and as a result, she came across in a way that made others feel inadequate and resentful, especially when they were performing tasks the way they liked to do them. We concluded our conversation on a much better note. She and I worked on some ideas for how she could modify her approach with the team.

That incident was just one of several I had in my career when having the confidence to speak up and call upon my ability to be empathetic and supportive while addressing an issue ultimately turned bad situations into much better ones. Sometimes, you have to understand the other person's point of view before making assumptions, and sometimes, the other person doesn't even realize they're coming across a certain way.

Having the confidence to speak up when ideas need to be shared or conflict needs to be resolved is a huge plus for any executive assistant who wants to be seen as a strategic business partner to the executive they support.

Successfully resolving conflict also requires connecting with that person in an amicable way so both parties are good once the issue has been discussed.

I never wanted to have conflict with other executive assistants on our team, but there were certainly occasions when one of them called me on something I did. I tended to be a bull in a china shop and could run over people with my ideas and enthusiasm at times, and yes, I had to be made aware of this. Their confidence in speaking up with me is what I was most proud of in some of the executive assistants on our team.

When a member of our executive assistant team sent me an email on a Friday to share her frustration with the way I was managing a certain project, at first I got defensive. "How dare she call me out on this after the fact?" I thought, and I must have read her email a dozen times with my blood pressure going through the roof the whole time. Then, I did what I would typically do and wrote a reply with all the harsh and defensive words I could muster. I didn't send that email, but writing it released all the negative energy. I took a step back and decided that email wasn't the way to get the situation back on track. I decided to apply the DFAA formula and write out my script for this situation.

I was introduced to this formula when I attended a weekend team-building seminar several years prior and found it tremendously useful in having direct conversations when there are issues to address. It works like this:

D: Describe the situation frustrating me in terms of "I" instead of "you." *I was caught by surprise, and I was so saddened by what I read.*

F: Facts. *This past Friday afternoon, I received the email, noting my failure to inform the team of a decision I had made.*

A: Action requested from the other person. *When I do something like this again, it would be great if I am called on it right away so I can course correct.*

A: Agreement. I ended my script with: *How can we get this back on track?*

I emailed her with a suggestion that we should probably meet in person and discuss her concerns, and she immediately replied that meeting would be okay with her. I had to think about the situation over the weekend and determine how best to handle it. I read her email again, picking apart specific statements she had made that I wanted to discuss with her.

Monday came, and I was ready. Again, mustering up my confidence, I approached her and let her know I was ready to discuss her email with her. We went into a private office, and I approached her email with a desire to understand what her comments meant. It was truly an eye-opening session for me. As she explained her feelings to me, I realized I hadn't taken certain things into consideration during our team meetings. I was driving for results that the team hadn't agreed to set as our goals. She was absolutely right that I was making certain decisions for the team, such as what methods we should use to roll out our newest initiative, and not getting everyone's buy-in, a real no-no for team members. Going forward, I would poll everyone on the team and call for their input before jumping ahead.

It was a humbling experience for me, but once we hashed it out, I apologized for my lack of awareness. We hugged each other, and she said something I will never forget: "We should have more conversations like this in the future." I owe a lot of my deep and lasting friendships with those executive assistants on our broad executive team to my abilities to listen, understand, communicate effectively with confidence, and accept feedback constructively.

Strained relationships and unresolved issues could diminish my abilities as an executive assistant supporting a CEO, so it was really important for me to develop my communication skills and emotional intelligence to quickly handle some of these situations in order to maintain a positive energy. That's the one thing I can say John was full of, positive energy. Every morning, he walked into our offices with this amazing energy, saying hi to anyone on the floor and popping his head into various executives' offices, and then he would come directly to my desk. It was like watching a tornado approach when you had nowhere to hide! I felt that electricity as soon as he passed me, giving me some kind of action item or a phone call he needed to make as he went. Grabbing my pad and pen, I ran after him to make sure I got everything right.

This was his typical style, and it dawned on me that it made his leadership unique. It was hard for me not to draw that energy into the many actions and responsibilities I had each day, and it made me realize the importance of bringing energy into the workplace. In our work environment, there were always challenges (and challenging people) to manage, but staying energetic brought about positivity and creativity and yes, even humor, not just from me, but from everyone else as well. It was far more fun to laugh than to get upset when I heard we had just decommissioned a technology tool I loved using and replaced it with a new one. I found the individuals working around me chiming in and adding additional humorous remarks, and soon, we were all laughing. It was a great stress relief.

Now, I wouldn't say that energy was easy to maintain, especially during somber times when there were reductions in workforce, reorganizations, and other company changes. However, I kept little tools at my desk to remind me to focus on bringing up the energy in times like those, like funny quotes, pictures of smiles, and a coffee cup with a quote that read: "Dream big. Get sh*t done. Have fun." (Thank you, Amy at LinkedIn). Some days, I felt the need to get creative with generating energy in the group around me.

One day, our company announced a reduction in workforce. The press was eating us alive about it, and everyone was heads-down, just intense, and worse, it was way too quiet. I had noticed a small ficus tree in the corner. (This was back when we had living plants in our offices). The spirit had long since left the tree; yellow and brown leaves scattered around the basket it sat in. I had been eyeing this tree for some weeks, and the leaves remained scattered around its base, so apparently, even our janitorial service had decided to ignore it. That's when I got this brilliant (at least I thought it was) idea. I got up from my desk, walked over to the pot, and began to pull the leaves together in a pile. At this point, one or two people in our area started watching. I carried my little pile of leaves over to my desk area and neatly placed it in front of my desk. Then, I promptly went back around to my computer and started working.

Several people were watching this, and finally, one of them just couldn't contain their curiosity any longer and asked me, "What are you doing? What is that pile of leaves for?" Then, everyone looked up from their computers. I said, "Let me show you!" (I was tickled that my co-worker had asked). I walked back around my desk and continued to walk down the hall away from the desk and the onlookers. I could hear comments from behind me. Someone said, "She's gone nuts. The job or John has gotten to her." When I was about twenty feet away from the area, I suddenly turned and started to sprint back to my desk. In one fell swoop, I plowed into the pile of leaves, scattering them in every different direction. The group was standing up and laughing at me. Mission accomplished. Our entire group's energy was up, there were smiles, and some head shaking, but in general, the atmosphere became positive. It was no longer quiet.

I came to know that, as leaders and strong strategic business partners, it was not only healthy but vital to bring a positive energy into the office every day and to expand that positive energy around us to other employees.

One of the ideas that upped the mood for our team was an evolving whiteboard where we wrote some of John's favorite sayings like, "Are we having fun yet?" and "You know where I'm headed with this." Even funnier, John must have walked by that whiteboard every day, and we don't think he even saw what was written there. Then there was the traveling bust, an ugly bronze bust of John. Every month, it mysteriously ended up on someone's desk, and the rule was that you couldn't pass it on for a month. It was hysterical to watch that bust travel all over the floor, and eventually, it made its way to other floors too.

I had inspirational and humorous quotes that popped up on my calendar on a weekly basis. I kept various journals, including a gratitude journal and what I called my "Here's how my day is going to go" journal, where I would write things like: "Today, I am going to knock it out of the park," or "I'm going to stay calm, cool, and collected," which actually paid off one day when I got pulled over for a speeding ticket.

I have a ton of stories about how, as a team, we used laughter (and love) to change the mood and the environment. I learned from John that, in times of low morale, sensitive moods, and extreme tension, I had to remain steady as a rock and to be like a duck: above the water, smooth sailing, and underneath, paddling furiously. That became my goal, no easy feat given that I felt much of the strain. But as John's strategic business partner I had to keep the team's emotions from going downhill or sideways as much as possible. I maintained a positive, confident smile during some of the toughest days of my life, like when John announced he was stepping down from the CEO role, and I had to email hundreds of his partners, customers, and friends.

Employees watch leadership for all kinds of messages being communicated about the company through posture, tone of voice, and facial expressions. In the toughest of times, John never wavered from his positive stance. (As his partner, I believed in that too.) During the holidays, John was determined to get out there among our employees and spread his positive energy and holiday spirit to as many people in as many buildings as he could cover during the day. Guess who was his holiday elf? Yes, I wore the elf hat with bells and pulled Santa John's bag of candy in a red wagon from building to building and floor to floor, shouting "Santa John is here!" As much as I hated wearing that elf hat, these were actually very special moments in my partnership with John.

When we stopped to talk with employees, John sat on the edge of a desk as they gathered around him and said, "Ask me any question you like. I'll try to answer it, and if I can't, my Lady Elf will get the answer for you." He got some pretty tough questions throughout the day, and I noted the trends in those questions. The employees loved taking pictures with him in his Santa hat (and you can guess who was taking those pictures), and when we left an area, there was a positive vibe in our wake. This was such a valuable lesson for me as John's partner. I needed to carry that energy with me every day, stopping and talking to other employees, getting a pulse of what was going on, and leaving them in that positive-vibe wake.

MAKE THE PLAY

1. As a leader, I developed the confidence to speak up when ideas needed to be shared or conflict needed to be resolved on our team. It was a huge plus in resolving team disagreements, which wasn't always easy.

2. Emotional intelligence was key to successfully resolving conflict.

3. Working with a highly dynamic executive, I had to come to the office every day with positive energy. It was vital to my partnership with John and with the teams around me.

4. I loved to use humor to bring about a good team atmosphere and reduce stress for the team and for me.

5. That energy allowed me to get a feel for employee morale and leave a positive vibe in my wake.

14. RESILIENCE

When you're working for one of the fastest-growing technology companies in the world, if you don't have resilience, you'll ultimately drown in the waves of change. Resilience wasn't my strongest competency in the early to middle years of my career. The biggest challenge was that John made some of the changes that affected me on some level. I lived through a number of major organizational changes, such as moving from a consolidated engineering team to business units for separate technologies and products, moving manufacturing from in-house to outsourcing, and a number of other changes over my career.

One of the biggest changes Cisco went through, which completely tested my resilience, was the move to a collaborative workspace. I had heard about this kind of work environment through the ranks as certain buildings and their employees served as test subjects for the concept. And I was not hearing good things. However, I wasn't worried because they would never bring that kind of work environment into the executive building—never.

Well, they did. The first test wave of the collaborative workspace came to our building when they decided to lower the cube walls. Suddenly, you could see heads. I was appalled. I felt naked, and I could hear people's conversations. I made it known, on more than one occasion, that I thought the whole concept was nuts. One day, as I was ranting in our work area about how ridiculous the idea was, our communications manager, Kelly, walked up to me and said, "Debbie, get over it. This is the way things are going to be, so stop fighting it. Roll with it." I never forgot that comment. I was swimming upstream and was going to lose the battle no matter how I fought it.

Resilience is the ability to embrace change, go with, and actually ride, the flow.

That's exactly what I did. I asked our Workplace Resources team if a few other executive assistants and I could join their planning team and help. They were thrilled to have us. In fact, they were very nervous about starting the project, especially with the senior level executive assistants and their executive offices. As senior executive assistants, we had very high expectations. Take one queen bee and then add ten more who not only worked for demanding executives but who could also be just as demanding themselves and who had definite opinions. (And boy, did we share those!)

I soon embraced the collaborative workspace idea, and I came back from the meetings and talked about the exciting new things we would be receiving, like desks with adjustable height, ergonomic chairs, and more. I became the champion for change. Now, that is what I call resilience. John had approved and moved forward with the changes, and as his strategic partner, I had to get on board too.

Maintaining resilience wasn't always easy. Our engineering and IT teams were constantly modifying, replacing, or completely throwing out a tool that, as executive assistants, we relied on. Learning the new technology they introduced was like learning how to drive a new car with new bells and whistles. Oh, there were training modules you could view online to learn about the tool, but how many people actually read the manual that comes with a new car? The important thing for me was recognizing I needed to learn each tool, no matter how painful it was, because John would ultimately use it or expect me to.

Two new tools rocked our world: Webex and TelePresence. Webex became our new meeting platform, and eventually, TelePresence was our video meeting platform. Simple, right? Not to me, considering I was fielding hundreds of meetings per month and sometimes per week. Some of John's meetings were with individuals who didn't even know what Webex was. "Wow," I thought, "how about just using the conference call method?"

In any case, over time, the two technology platforms merged into one hairy monster. Suddenly, I was scheduling Webex/TP calls in John's office with customers across the globe and trying to figure out what technologies they had that would work with ours. Which platform worked, how they could share their presentations, which of John's direct TP numbers would connect right into his office, and what passcode and meeting number to use—the variables to consider went on and on. On more than one occasion, I thought everything was set up perfectly. John was sitting, ready for the meeting to begin, when unexpectedly, something went wrong. The list of the errors that occurred on any one TP session is just too long to explain. In some cases, we had IT teams on both sides of the technology to make sure the meeting ran smoothly. I gritted my teeth on more than occasion.

My resilience was definitely tested one day at a staff meeting I will never forget. John had invited all of his senior staff, as well as other members of the team, to a special senior staff meeting, where he was going to bring in a guest speaker. There were more than sixty people dialing in via Webex. I was on the edge of glass that day because I was nervous about the video that would be shown on our boardroom screen and because everyone also needed to be able to see and hear our presenter. People started arriving and asking me if there was any coffee, and I suddenly realized catering hadn't shown up yet. We were ten minutes away from the kickoff of the meeting.

I ran out of the room and called catering directly, only to be told they were a bit behind and would be there in less than five minutes. However, that didn't happen. John walked in with our guest speaker and began to introduce him to members of the staff. I was at my computer, ready to open the Webex lines for the remote guests, when I was pinged on my IM. Someone couldn't get in because the meeting number was invalid. I had no idea what was going on.

By then, John was seated. I was to his right, and our guest speaker was beginning his presentation. In the meantime, I was getting ping after ping after ping. No one could get in. John looked over at me with an expression that asked, "What's up?" I discreetly picked up my laptop and walked out of the room and to the nearest cubicle to call IT. I was desperate. The pinging wasn't stopping, and my cell phone was ringing too.

My call to IT support vibrated through the walls of the entire building. I was a woman on fire, soon to burn and take everyone down with me. IT answered, and they were calmly discussing the issue, but I finally screamed into the phone, "Stop! I don't care what caused the issue. I just want it fixed now!" I almost never raised my voice to anyone, let alone to my favorite team, IT, but I felt the noose tightening around my neck. I was going to be hanged if I didn't get those sixty people into that room via Webex.

At light speed, they fixed my issue with a new meeting number, and I blasted that out to the sixty remotes. Then, I softly walked back into the staff room to sit down next to John. The guest presenter was speaking and making a great connection with the staff. John looked at me with a less-than-warm look, but things were back on track. My blood pressure was starting to subside when the door to the boardroom opened and in walked catering with coffee, pastries, sodas, and waters. (What happened to five minutes?) At this point, the speaker stopped his presentation, and John gave me a look that said, "We're gonna talk after this meeting." In his calm way, John laughed and told the attendees and the speaker we would take a five-minute break so people could grab some coffee or run to the restroom.

I was beyond mortified, and I just knew I was going to need to start drafting my resignation letter. Finally, catering left, the speaker resumed, all sixty remotes were on, and the meeting was ultimately successful. After the meeting, I was wishing I was under the boardroom table as the executives filed out. One of the VPs walked over to me, handed me a tissue, and said with a smile, "I thought you might need this." He patted me on the back and left the room. Needless to say, I didn't quite go with the flow that day. John didn't reprimand me or fire me, but he did provide some guidance about always planning ahead for the worst-case scenario so I could be ready if it happened.

I adopted the mindset that, when stuff happens, I need to manage through it and just go with the flow, riding with it the way you're supposed to ride with the water when you get sucked in by a riptide. I also started to use post-mortems with the teams behind the scenes to find out how we could improve—what went great and what went wrong. Resilience is not just adapting but also improving.

 MAKE THE PLAY

1. Resilience required me to stop fighting against change because that wasn't going to work. As much as I disliked some changes, I needed to move with them.

2. I had to develop the ability to embrace the change and even ask to be part of it by joining the teams making the changes.

3. I became the champion for change.

4. I had to learn new tools that were part of change, no matter

how painful, because my role supporting John required it.

5. It became important to me to always plan ahead for the worst-case scenarios so I could be ready if they did happen.

6. I adopted the mindset that when "stuff" happens, I need to manage through it and just go with the flow.

7. I used post-mortems with the teams behind the scenes to find out how we could improve. Continuous improvement is a part of resilience.

15. WHAT'S NEXT?

The day finally came, in March of 2016, when my world changed yet again. The Cisco board had been discussing succession planning with John for quite a while, and it was only a matter of time. My own thoughts had been shifting too. What would I do once my role as John's chief executive assistant and my reign in the administrative community came to an end?

You might think I was scared, nervous, or fearful of that "what next" question. I was. I didn't kid myself. I was queen of all I surveyed. I had unbelievable power to make things happen. I was working for one of the most amazing CEOs in the world. I was doing what I loved, training administrative professionals within Cisco and externally and living life large. What really scared me was losing all of that and not knowing what my new path would look like.

I was asked to assist in planning an offsite board meeting that was to take place in Half Moon Bay, California. The word "offsite" to me implied sessions on strategy and vision planning. This particular meeting would include three of our senior executive vice presidents who were scheduled to meet individually with the board over the three days. There definitely was some strategy planning in process. Like a stone dropped in a pond, I had a feeling that the ripple effect would eventually touch me.

I was well aware of the reasons behind the offsite, a highly confidential session where key Cisco executives would be brought in to interview for the CEO role. It was essential that no one outside the board members know of the succession plans taking place. I was one of the privileged few who attended and supported the meeting, but what would happen over those two and a half days hadn't really sunk in for me.

I sat with our security director at the little table (the kids' table) outside the conference room, waiting for the next ask from a board member. These special requests included things like, "Can you bring in an espresso and cappuccino machine? The hotel coffee is too weak." Or "Absolutely no chardonnay at dinner, only the finest sauvignon blanc," a request which came after I had everyone seated at the dinner table. Just call me Debbie "Ready for Anything!"

Well, "anything" happened. One of the board members asked me for help in orchestrating a special marriage proposal to his girlfriend, who had traveled with him and was staying at the hotel. He wanted to propose to her as the sun set over the ocean with bagpipes playing in the background and the engagement ring on a silver appetizer tray. I'm no wedding planner (thank goodness), but I went into action. The sun would set at five in the evening, and I only had a day to work everything out.

I immediately connected with the hotel sales lead, who was our lead contact for our board meeting, and we combined forces. She secured the bagpiper, and I went off to deal with catering. I needed the perfect small appetizer dish and a waiter to deliver it. All at five o'clock on the dot. At four o'clock, the soon-to-be-married couple was sitting out on the lawn deck of the hotel, holding hands and looking at the ocean, two champagne glasses on their table. At exactly 4:58, I signaled the bagpiper to start playing. As the sun started to set, up walked the waiter with the silver service dish. The look on the girlfriend's face was priceless. Smartphone cameras went off as people who didn't even know these two witnessed the amazing moment. Another miracle pulled off.

The next day, I was staring at the ocean instead of my emails, thinking about how beautiful the marriage proposal had been the night before, when John came out of the conference room and asked me to take a walk. Sitting across from me in an empty conference room down the hall, he shared that there would be a new CEO in Cisco town. The change would be announced in May. My first reaction was actually no reaction. John let me know that we would be fine and that he would take care of me when the change was made official. He even indicated that, depending on what his next moves were, there could possibly be a place for me to support him.

I knew the change would happen, but you're never fully prepared for it. The news hadn't sunk in yet when one of the board members gave me a huge hug and asked me what I planned to do next.

Then an executive assistant arriving on site with paperwork for one of the board members asked me the same question. Was this happening tomorrow? Should I have packed up my desk ahead of time? Would my desk even be waiting for me when I returned, or would I find someone else sitting there? I had a nightmare that evening about walking into the Cisco office to find my desk wasn't where it usually was. I was lost, and no one even knew who I was.

Knowing things were changing, I just buried my head in the sand for awhile. I felt safer that way.

I didn't know what tomorrow would look like, nor did I have a plan, but change was coming, like a huge wave off in the distance.

Reality hit a short time later when John provided me a list of everyone he'd ever known in the world who he wanted to email with his personal announcement of his pending title change to chairman emeritus. Every day, day in and day out, for almost a week, I emailed his partners, customers, friends, and peers, and the government officials with whom he had relationships. My fingers were cramping and my heart was sinking.

It was really happening.

I loved being able to creatively bring administrative teams together through the years as John's executive assistant. It had been great to grow up with so many wonderful executives, who I watched being promoted from managers to directors and vice presidents, some of whom I coached or provided insights to along the way. I loved being able to teach and mentor the administrative assistants who were now so much a part of me. I loved traveling to amazing places, like Italy, Zurich, and even India with John or on my own as Cisco's Chief Executive Assistant. I enjoyed participating in fantastic Cisco events and hearing wonderful and inspirational speakers, including John. There would be a huge hole left in my heart when my reign was officially over.

Once the word was out, I was peppered with questions from people within the company. *What are you going to do now? Are you going to stay with Cisco? Are you going to stay with John?* As I was thinking of my next move, it saddened me to see people shift their allegiances to new management. I felt somewhat out of the loop with communications coming and going from the new CEO's office. Although that wasn't a bad thing, I was no longer as in the know as I had been. The newer executives coming in didn't ask for my guidance in terms of who or what they should look for in an executive assistant. I felt I was becoming obsolete.

Then in May, it was officially announced. John would be stepping down from the chairman and CEO role and handing over his reign to our new CEO. There were press interviews and employee communications about the transfer of power. It was surreal and it was real. Slowly, the transformation began. John's responsibilities evolved from the daily running of the business to a concentrated focus on global digitization and a keen interest in innovation and startups. He became the president of the India Business Council, a huge undertaking, just when I thought things would slow down a bit. However, slowing down was definitely not John's style. He was embracing the change and putting his energies into doing new things, where he felt he could truly make a difference.

It was time I did the same.

John's interest in innovation and investment in the startup world became one of his passions. It meant John's office became a revolving door of young startup CEOs, coming and going. Once again, I had to shift my thinking and my processes based on his new priorities. I created new briefing templates that captured the information John wanted to know, from who the startup's investors were to how many employees they had and what their products or services were. Google became a dear friend of mine during this time as I constantly researched the companies and the people. I had to learn which startups he had an interest in and which ones wouldn't make it past my email or phone.

We were in an onslaught of outreaches once the word got out that John was investing. Not only was he investing, but he was also joining the startup boards as an advisor. He was on four or five startup boards within just a few months, and I was drowning in a whole new way. My executive assistant team, which once consisted of four of us, was whittled down to just my last trusted partner, Dorothea, and me. The workload, while it shifted, was just about the same—a lot.

I felt like a mother hen managing these young startup CEOs who had no concept of what working with a big corporate type, like John, required. Briefings I requested for meetings with John were scorned. The only way to reach some of these CEOs was by texting. Their own executive assistants wore many hats too, so getting timely information from them for John could be difficult at best. The sense of urgency varied from young company to young company. My patience was tested.

On one occasion, I knew John had one of his startup board meetings coming up, and as was typical, I required all the board materials be in John's hands in advance of the board meeting so he could prepare. The CEO's executive assistant and I communicated, and I asked her when we could see the board materials, to which she promptly said, "You'll have it tomorrow by noon." That was the day before John was to fly out to meet with the board members, and I was a little nervous. I had lots of tabs to make and paperwork to stuff into the board binder, but I could handle it. The next day, I had nothing from the startup at noon and nothing at two o'clock. I emailed the executive assistant and, in a panic, tried to call her. Alas, I still had nothing from her at four o'clock in the afternoon, and I was losing my mind.

At five o'clock, I received an email from the executive assistant, which said, "Oh, the board material was sent by our CEO this morning to John's email, and he should have it by now." Was she kidding me? Where was the call indicating the information was in John's inbox that morning? While I checked John's emails fairly regularly, I was buried and hadn't had a chance to check it again. How did she miss the panic and frustration in my voice and my desperate email? This was Executive Assistant Etiquette 101.

It was going to be a long night, and my emotional intelligence was in the tank. These were very bright young people, and they were excited about their future working with John on their startup. I always thought I was bright too (although not as young), but I wasn't so excited about my future working with John. He was creating his own venture capital firm behind the scenes. I was going gray quickly. It was time for me to start planning my next move.

My role was changing. I watched the new CEO's assistant from where I sat, realizing all I could do was give guidance if she asked for it. I was only asked for it once in that final year. The new CEO's assistant was trying so hard to make everyone like her as she took on her new role. She was struggling with one of the executive assistants on her team, someone who had no concept of budgets, especially when it came to hosting amazing events. And these events were truly amazing. From baristas pouring wonderful coffees for a breakfast get-together to smoked salmon and caviar appetizers for staff meetings.

The CEO's assistant was humble, gracious, and too nice. My one piece of advice to her was this: "While it's important to build good relationships in your role, you must always do what's right for the business first. If someone isn't adhering to the policies or procedures as mandated by your CEO, you need to step up and speak to that person. It's not about being friends. It's about doing what's right for the business." I'm not sure she ever really addressed the issue. The events were still amazing until the day I departed.

I felt my ability to make a difference (my power) was slipping away every day I sat there at my desk. I was no longer leading, and I sadly watched some of the greatest initiatives my teams and I had worked on and implemented over many years, such as the annual All Hands Administrative Meeting and the Administrative Professionals Performance Assessment, which determined if an administrative assistant was ready for promotion based on skill-level ratings, face a slow death. It was sad, and it was frustrating for me. Where were the existing executive assistants who would take the lead to keep these initiatives thriving? I wanted to vent, but alas, everyone was heads-down and managing through the changes. As for me, I wasn't head-down, but my head was definitely lowered.

I wasn't sure, but I sensed John was feeling the same way I did. We just weren't needed any longer. My favorite thing to say to John during this time was: "John, we are now the parents in the newlyweds' home, and we should probably move out," to which he would laugh with that twinkle in his eye. It was definitely time for me to initiate my own next chapter. It was time to move on.

Many people have asked me why I didn't decide to go with John in his new chapter in life, and I will tell you straight out. I was tired! Working for a man who moved at light speed, like a two-year-old on candy, every day for twenty-six years, had worn me out.

But there was another reason I decided not to follow John. I had grown to love mentoring, coaching, and training administrative professionals to achieve excellence throughout my Cisco career and felt I had found my passion.

When you find your passion, you will know it. It's what you do and lose all track of time while you're doing it.

I didn't want to lose the opportunity that had been given me by the higher divine power. I believed I was meant to truly make a difference in other people's lives. I had already been successfully doing that for John, and now, it was my turn.

Teaching and training administrative professionals was like food for my soul, and I knew it was the direction I wanted to take once John officially retired from Cisco. I had actually been thinking about doing this for several years before I even knew what John's retirement date would be. I had coached individual Cisco administrative professionals, assisting them in getting out of their comfort zones to do incredible things, and I had trained hundreds and hundreds of Cisco's administrative professionals in new ways of thinking and being.

I did not want to give that up.

I started packing up my world in late November, before Thanksgiving of 2017. What a way to continually remind myself how thankful I was for the career I had with Cisco and with John. I cleaned out files filled with great memories that pulled at my heartstrings and gave away my favorite tchotchkes, which held places of honor on my desk, to my favorite people. This included a jar that sat on my counter with a label that read: "Ashes of Idiots." This jar had become well known by all. If someone managed to piss me off, to keep my temper in check, I would write a little note about what the person did to anger me and then fold it up and put it in that jar. Let's just say quite a few notes went in that jar over the years.

As the days started to get closer to John's last board meeting, on December 17th, my desk was fairly empty and wiped clean of the "Debbie Gross" brand. My bookshelf held no books. My sources of knowledge and inspiration and motivation were safely packed away. John's office was just as bare, as we had been packing up his personal things for weeks. Then there were the storerooms, where more of his belongings resided. It was a huge undertaking to sort through and pack more than twenty-six years of stuff, so many memories stored in files and boxes. Every day was liking walking down memory lane as I either threw an item out or boxed it up to take home. Having collected so much stuff over our many years at Cisco, in some ways it felt like cleaning out a closet with things you don't need, use, or want, and finding that one thing you'd forgotten about that you just can't bear to part with.

I got some sad looks from people as they walked by and saw my almost empty desk. I was going to miss these people who had been my family for twenty-six years, and I could see they sure as hell were going to miss me. "What are we going to do without you here?" they asked. "We're going to miss hearing you and John laugh," they said. I was a light that would soon fade on the fifth floor of building 10.

I had one last thing I needed to do in order to make my transition out of Cisco complete. I was going to wipe clean the whiteboard in John's office. This was no ordinary whiteboard, folks. This was a floor-to-ceiling, fifteen-foot whiteboard wall. It was covered from top to bottom with notes, drawings, concepts, ideas, and strategies that either John or people who met with him had written there. John did not allow anyone to erase that board. It was a work of art.

I took a picture of the board, and then I got to work. My partner poked her head in from time to time to ask me if I needed help, and

I said no. I was determined that it would be me who cleaned this slate. Slightly lightheaded from the cleaner, I stood there amongst the mounds of colorfully stained paper towels on the floor and finally surveyed the completely clean white wall. I had closed out an era.

On Thursday, December 17, 2017, after John's final board meeting, he, our core team, and I walked towards the elevator that would take us down to the lobby. We rode down together quietly—Dorothea, my partner; John and his two communications managers, Kelsey and Shannon; and me. Either it was smoky in there, or there was mist in our eyes. When we arrived at the lobby, there was a huge line of employees waiting to say goodbye. There were many, many hugs and tears too.

John and I walked out of those Cisco doors at 300 E. Tasman Drive, turned back, and waved goodbye. Then he and I hugged each other and high-fived. "Well done!" he said, and each of us rode off into the sunset, going our separate ways.

The next chapter for both of us had begun.

MAKE THE PLAY

1. I knew that change was coming, but I kept my head buried in the sand. It seemed like the safe thing to do, but it meant I wasn't prepared. Playing it safe is giving in to fear, which can rule our thoughts.

2. I decided to pull my head up, embrace the change, and put my energies into doing things where I could effect change, be in charge of the changes, and not let them rule me.

3. I shifted my thinking and modified or created new processes based on John's new priorities.

4. I saw where my true passion lay. It went beyond supporting John. It was the one thing I could do and lose all track of time doing it. I found joy and inspiration in teaching other administrative professionals to become stars. Never ignore your passion when it shows itself.

16. DEBBIE GROSS — THE GRAND OPENING!

I t has been almost two years since that December 2017 day, and boy, has my growth and development continued. Sharing stories of my amazing career and the lessons I learned along the way has been a great journey for me so far, and believe me, I have more yet to tell.

Now, it's time to tell an entirely new story.

It's the grand opening of Debbie Gross! I'm focusing my full attention on serving as an advocate for the administrative profession, sharing insights and passion about what it takes to create excellence in the role.

I had the ideal career as Chief Executive Assistant, working for an amazing CEO and making a great income. Why did I leave the executive assistant profession when I could have continued down that path? I listened to my inner voice. While working at Cisco and also at UCSC Extension in Santa Clara, I taught and mentored thousands of administrative professionals. I discovered that my true passion and purpose is teaching and inspiring other people in the administrative profession to be the absolute best they can be.

In this next chapter of my life, my strongest desire is to see the profession recognized, to have the world acknowledge that this is much more than just a support position. It's a powerful role that should be highly valued and recognized by management the way my own executive valued me. The key to a company's overall success is operational excellence, which means having well-trained and highly motivated administrative professionals working at their best. I learned from the best and became the best, and I have helped thousands of administrative professionals around the world achieve recognized strategic partnerships with their principals. I know I can show you how it's done.

When you walk into my shop of knowledge, you won't find shoes, accessories, or the latest fashions. Instead, you will get a sense that there's real inspiration and passion in the air. You'll see in the window the model of what an exceptional and valued executive assistant looks like. You'll find many examples of best practices, tips, and strategies that I developed and which work in real life. These tools made me successful over twenty-six years of working for one of the most demanding, fast-moving, detail-oriented executives in the corporate world.

As the proprietor of this shop, I share all the gifts I received throughout my years as an executive assistant, from time management to communication skills and strategic thinking. Remaining steadfast and dependable, I am a committed coach and advocate for the profession. I am a guide to take others out of their comfort zones. On my shop counters, you will see my specialties: encouragement, motivation, confidence-building, and creativity-sparking!

But wait. There's more!

When you leave, you will have a new voice. One that speaks up with confidence. Any anxiety and self-doubt will have dissipated. You will be considered a valued member of the team as you use the tools you have been given. You will think strategically and communicate effectively. Your management team will recognize the tremendous value you bring to them.

A note from one of my students who now exemplifies administrative excellence:

Dear Debbie,

I want to express my appreciation for you. I am and will always be grateful. You saw something in me that makes me the person I am today! The memory of our first meeting is still fresh in my heart and mind. I was thinking to myself how lucky all the people are who get coaching from you, and then, because you believed in me and took me under your wing, here I am today, from just a job to a real career. The unstoppable me.
Deepika
Executive Assistant
Collinear Networks, Inc.

Welcome to my grand opening! Come on in and take a look around at **debbiegross.com**. You just might find the career of your dreams!

ACKNOWLEDGMENTS

I'm not sure this book would have ever been written or even finished if it weren't for some key people in my life who helped me realize my passion and purpose—and who helped me to see my dreams come true.

First and foremost, I want to acknowledge my mom and dad, Judy and Aubrey. Thank you for bringing me into this world (feet first) and teaching me the importance of love and patience in a sometimes messy life. I also have to thank my sister Teresa who, as I grew up, I thought was a bit of a pain in my side as sisters can be, but who eventually became my best friend and advocate—especially during the tough times. She continually encouraged me, shared her admiration of me, and told me she thought I was a great writer and to keep at it. Thank you, sis.

A huge thank-you to my husband, Cory, who took a leap of faith when he asked me to marry him and who has put up with my long work hours, my moods, my challenges, as well as my successes, and who remains forever the foundation that keeps me grounded.

It can sometimes be a lonely and arduous road when one starts a new chapter in life and even more so when deciding to write a book, so I have to thank two of my very best friends for being there for me: Mimi and Jenny. I often tease Mimi that she was the other sister hidden in the attic because she, my sister and I just bonded right off the bat. (She even looks like me.) Mimi has always been there for me when I have been stressed or just feeling blue, making me laugh by wearing one of her many funny costumes and always pulling me back into a positive state. Thank you, Mimi, for your infectious enthusiasm and for showing me that life can be fun!

Then there is Jenny, whom I actually interviewed for a sales assistant's role back in my early twenties. She was just eighteen years old and I wasn't sure she would be mature enough for the job (I was only four years older); however, we took a chance on hiring her and she became one of my best friends. She was the person who actually opened the door for me to eventually become an executive assistant. Because of her, I ended up with one of the best careers I have ever had, as an Executive Assistant for one of the most dynamic and amazing CEOs in the world. She has always believed in me and my capabilities to inspire and motivate others.

I also have to acknowledge the wonderful administrative community at Cisco, which embraced me with love and respect and showed me the impact of my inspiration and teaching, as they became unbelievable "Office Rockstars." Love all of you!

It was Celeste, Cisco's HR program manager, who pushed me out of my comfort zone and got me in front of Cisco's newly hired administrators to share the Cisco culture. I would never have found my passion for teaching if she hadn't seen my potential, so a huge thank-you goes out to her. I definitely can't forget my presentation coach, Jeff, who showed me that giving a presentation in front of an audience can actually be fun.

I have to thank Joan, CEO of Office Dynamics International, who certified me to teach her amazing administrative training programs and to live and breathe my passion for teaching, and who strongly encouraged me to write this book.

One of the most important people in my life who brought out the true "Office Rockstar" in me was John Chambers. His wisdom and vision for me changed my thinking about writing this book. Our partnership of more than twenty-six years taught me so many valuable lessons, and John persuasively urged me to write about them. Watching and learning from him helped me become the person I am today in so many ways. He is an amazing advisor, teacher, and above all, a dear friend.

I'm sure there are so many others out there who were part of this journey of mine, including all of my students. So with that, I'm sending a heartfelt "thank-you" to all of you who have played such a vital part in my life and helped me realize my passion and my dream.

ABOUT THE AUTHOR

Debbie Gross knows that administrative excellence is about more than juggling schedules and taking notes. An intuitive leader, she offers a fresh approach to teaching administrative professionals how to upgrade their soft skills and build confidence. Whether on stage or in the classroom, she has an innate ability to transform staff into leaders, drawing out the inner "Office Rockstar."

As the former Chief Executive Assistant to John Chambers, the past CEO of Cisco (a global corporation based in Silicon Valley), Debbie supported the company's growth from a multimillion-dollar business to a multibillion-dollar enterprise. Known as John's "right hand," she increased his productivity by 40 percent. Debbie designed initiatives and programs that helped the global administrative community at Cisco grow and thrive. Now, she's using her thirty years of experience to help the next generation of administrative professionals transition from overwhelmed task managers to strategic business partners.

She's conducted interactive workshops and motivational talks at companies such as Cisco, Veritas, Facebook, Fenwick & West, and FedEx. Debbie doesn't just share information—she inspires and incites greatness. Her distinctive teaching style blends creativity, fun, and new thought processes to help administrative professionals gain greater career satisfaction, recognition, and promotions.

For her passion and advocacy, the Admin Awards of Silicon Valley presented her with the Colleen Barrett Award, the highest recognition given for administrative excellence.

Originally from Jackson, Mississippi, Debbie currently lives in Campbell, CA with her husband, Cory.

Interested in having me speak or train at your organization? Here are my core topics:

- Creating Successful Business Partnerships
- The Wow Factor: Communicating for Successful Outcomes
- Rev Up Your Brand: Executive Presence!
- The Résumé That Gets Results
- Building a Great Team: The Recipe for Organizational Success
- Communicating with Confidence
- Time Management
- Managing the Executive's Calendar: The Great Challenge!
- The Art of Influence When You Have No Authority
- Interviewing to Impress
- Administrative Excellence: Become Recognized and Indispensable

I also offer one-on-one coaching for executive-level assistants. Contact me for details.

LET'S CONNECT!

web: debbiegross.com
email: debbie@debbiegross.com
phone: (408) 442-8922
on social: **@winwithdebbieg**

A FREE GIFT
FOR YOU!

Are You Ready to Achieve Your Dream Career?

Download this guide to learn how to:
- Remain relaxed and prepared for tough questions
- Impress your interviewer by learning the questions you should ask
- Distinguish yourself from other candidates so they will hire *you*
- Appear the expert by learning what *not* to say

and more!

DOWNLOAD YOUR FREE GUIDE TODAY!
www.debbiegrosscareertips.com

Made in United States
North Haven, CT
05 October 2022